Saturday Night Believer

Stories of Music Ministry from the Front Line

Saturday Night Believer

Stories of Music Ministry from the Front Line

Scott Fellows

BOOKS

Winchester, UK
Washington, USA

First published by O-Books, 2010
O Books is an imprint of John Hunt Publishing Ltd., The Bothy, Deershot Lodge, Park Lane, Ropley,
Hants, SO24 0BE, UK
office1@o-books.net
www.o-books.com

Distribution in:	South Africa
	Stephan Phillips (pty) Ltd
UK and Europe	Email: orders@stephanphillips.com
Orca Book Services Ltd	Tel: 27 21 4489839 Telefax: 27 21 4479879
Home trade orders	Text copyright Scott Fellows 2010
tradeorders@orcabookservices.co.uk	
Tel: 01235 465521 Fax: 01235 465555	ISBN: 978 1 84694 415 4
Export orders	Design: Tom Davies
exportorders@orcabookservices.co.uk	
Tel: 01235 465516 or 01235 465517	All rights reserved. Except for brief quotations
Fax: 01235 465555	in critical articles or reviews, no part of this
	book may be reproduced in any manner
USA and Canada	without prior written permission from the
NBN	publishers.
custserv@nbnbooks.com	
Tel: 1 800 462 6420 Fax: 1 800 338 4550	The rights of Scott Fellows as author have
	been asserted in accordance with the
Australia and New Zealand	Copyright, Designs and Patents Act 1988.
Brumby Books	
sales@brumbybooks.com.au	A CIP catalogue record for this book is
Tel: 61 3 9761 5535 Fax: 61 3 9761 7095	available from the British Library.
Far East (offices in Singapore, Thailand,	
Hong Kong, Taiwan)	
Pansing Distribution Pte Ltd	Printed in the UK by CPI Antony Rowe
kemal@pansing.com	Printed in the USA by Offset Paperback Mfrs,
Tel: 65 6319 9939 Fax: 65 6462 5761	Inc

We operate a distinctive and ethical publishing philosophy in all
areas of its business, from its global network of authors to
production and worldwide distribution.

CONTENTS

Acknowledgements

My thanks go to:
Band members over the years who made 'Freedom' work.
To the landlords and concert secretaries who took a chance on us.

To the unsuspecting Ministers, Chaplains and Church Secretaries who invited us into their fellowships

To all those who helped us in practical ways, from stuffing envelopes to carrying gear, from providing rehearsal space to donating money

To our fellow performers and musicians who encouraged us and helped us.

To all those who prayed for our ministry

To friends who read parts of this book in its development and helped with suggestions.

To our wives and husbands, boyfriends, girlfriends and families who supported us and put up with all the late finishes and early starts, all the moaning and the traumas, the triumphs and the tragedies, the histrionics and hysteria and the hours and hours of practicing tricky chord changes deep into the night.

And last but not least to all the pub goers, club members and congregations who were ready to politely listen (in spite of everything).

Preface

If you enjoy reading books that give you an honest, warts and all, behind the scenes look at the lives of the rich and famous, then this book is for you; as long as you leave out the 'rich and famous' part.

This is the story of a Christian rock band that was never signed to a record label, never appeared on main stage at a big music festival (in spite of the picture on the cover) and never bothered the music charts, even the Christian ones. It's the story of ordinary Christians, with a medium helping of musical talent, who spent 20 years or so performing all over the north of England entirely undetected by music industry radar.

In 1995 Cross Rhythms magazine, one of the then UK's foremost Christian music magazines, reviewed one of our albums "New Street" thus:

> One could surely be forgiven for expecting someone with a voice like Scott Fellows to hail from Las Vegas. Nothing is lost, however, to discover he resides in Stockport. With a vocal style on 'New Street' reminiscent of classic 60's cabaret singers like Tony Christie…they have recorded a range of material, from white soul duets to mellow jazz cabaret numbers that evoke a smoky nightclub opulence…12 original tracks written by Fellows, with flawlessly professional arrangements and production, it will perhaps find its warmest reception amongst the generation for which a three-course meal, smart attire, and a taxi to The Roxy is still a Saturday night to be savoured. Why such a class act are not signed to a label one can only wonder.

A nice review but you've probably spotted the key phrase here, it's in the last line: 'not signed to a label'.

Why then bother to part with hard earned cash to purchase this book and read about such a band, that never hit the 'big time'? Well our experiences were down to earth and real, sometimes painfully so. We made lots of mistakes along the way as well as the occasional good decision but, here's the thing, we found God working in *every* situation, even the seemingly hopeless ones. So if you have ever wondered whether God is still active in our modern world, whether He has time for *ordinary* people like you and me and, just now and then, whether He has a sense of humour...read on.

All the events and characters depicted in this book are real, some names have been changed for reasons of privacy and the sequence of some events adjusted to ease the narrative flow.

Chapter 1: The Beginning

As I put my key in my front door lock I immediately sensed something was wrong. I had been to a party that evening and was a little worse for wear, it was nearly three in the morning. As the door swung open and I stepped inside the hallway, my suspicion turned to certainty. I walked the few steps in darkness to the hall light switch, I could hear my footsteps echo off the walls, the floor felt different underfoot, it felt harder. I flicked the switch, completely unprepared for the shock ahead.

The hall was empty, no, it was more than empty, it was stripped bare. The furniture, the hatstand, the wooden cupboard that the phone sat on, the big vase of flowers that stood on the floor in the corner, all gone. I looked down and suddenly realized why my footsteps had echoed, the carpet had gone too. I stood for a moment, unable to take in the scene, to understand what it meant, then panic gripped me and I rushed from room to room, turning on lights all over the house, running up and down the stairs. Every room told the same story, stripped of all possessions, furniture and carpets gone. All that was left was a bed, just the frame and mattress; some of my books and records, in piles on the floor; and my clothes, laying across the bed. I wandered around the house for at least half an hour, checking the same rooms over and over, just in case it wasn't real somehow. At last, physically and mentally exhausted, I sat cross legged on the floorboards of the living room. Above my head a naked light bulb threw its merciless light into every bare corner. I sat motionless, my mind was in turmoil. I knew who was responsible for this and I knew what I was going to do about it. I jumped to my feet.

I threw my car around the side streets of my estate as if I was driving in a Grand Prix. I hit the open road and pushed my foot to the metal. I couldn't give a damn about my speed, tears of pain and fury blurred my vision, my only thought was revenge. The first light of dawn spread across the sky as I hurtled towards my target. No light penetrated my darkness. By the time I pulled up outside my father-in-law's house, I was beside myself with rage. I jumped out of the car, ran up the drive and started hammering on the door and shouting at the top of my voice.

'Alf, Alf come on you b******, open the door.'

I crouched down to look through the letter box, dimly by the morning light I could see some of my stuff. I hammered again.

'Open the door Alf! I'm not going anywhere until I get my stuff back.'

I ran around the back of the house just in time to see my estranged wife standing at the window of her ground floor bedroom. She had gone back there after we had separated a few months before. Up to now things had been amicable between us, or so I had thought. Jill looked out at me through the glass, her face wore a lost expression This was not a face I could shout at, I still loved her and couldn't bring myself to believe that she had played a part in what had happened. Our eyes met through the window, there was only one thing I wanted to say to her.

'Why?'

She looked down, was it an act of embarrassment? I didn't know and I didn't get the chance to ask. Phone calls had been made and at that moment a policeman walked around the corner of the house, followed by Alf. Alf made sure that the policeman stayed between me and him, he pointed accusingly over the policeman's shoulder.

'There he is, I want him off my property. He's trespassing.'

I saw red, 'Trespassing? What about you, coming into my house and cleaning it out, that's trespassing and theft.' The policeman intervened.

'Look sir, why don't you calm down, get back in your car and go home. You're not going to sort out anything here are you?'

'This is ridiculous, I get my house ransacked and I'm the one who ends up getting lectured by the police.'

Over the policeman's shoulder I could see Alf's face, it had a smug look, the kind of look that provoked violence. I took a step toward him and found myself eyeball to eyeball with the law:

'Go home sir, now!'

Two years on from that night and the anger and bitterness had not left me. There was a quickie divorce to follow. I had never got any of my stuff back, as my solicitor had reminded me 'possession is nine tenths of the law'. My comfortable lifestyle in my comfortable home had collapsed, literally, overnight. When I discovered that Jill had stopped paying her half of the mortgage months before and that there were considerable arrears owing, I had been forced to take in lodgers to help pay the bills. My house resembled a second hand furniture shop and the expensive carpets I had proudly fitted when we had moved in to our new home were now replaced by cheap cord. I drank too much and spent long periods brooding on my own. It was one evening, during one of these brooding sessions, that the phone rang. I rarely bothered to answer the phone anymore, most of my friends had drifted away not able to deal with my unrelenting bitterness. The only phone calls I got these days were from over-excited youths telling me I'd won a free holiday or had been specially chosen, from hundreds of others in my area, to receive a discount on replacement windows. I didn't know why but this time something made me put my drink down, get up out of my chair and answer the phone.

'Scott?'

'Yes,' I didn't recognize the voice.

'It's Dave Longton. I don't know whether you remember me. We met briefly at Andy's house.' I dimly recalled. Andy was one of my few remaining friends, Dave had gone to school with Andy, the only thing I knew about him was that he played drums.

'I understand you've been going through a rough time lately.'

I was immediately on the defensive, I no longer trusted people's motives, I answered non-commitally.

'Oh yes.'

'Look, I don't want to push you but a group of us are going to a music festival and wondered if you'd like to join us.'

I had been a musician since I was a child, my curiosity was faintly aroused.

'What kind of music festival?' There was a slight pause at the other end, as if Dave was forming his answer carefully.

'A pop festival, open air, you'd sleep in a tent. It's great fun, we go every year with our church.'

Church? For a few moments I was confused, the pop festivals I'd been to didn't exactly seem churchy affairs, far from it. Then the penny dropped, they were trying to save me, the God Squad were on my case, I wasn't having any of that.

'It's good of you to offer Dave but I'm...' a moment's hesitation, 'I'm busy that weekend.' Dave's reply had a serious tone, 'I didn't mention the date.'

'Oh, I assumed you meant this coming weekend.'

'No, it's in three weeks' time.'

'Well, I think I've got something on then too unfortunately.'

'OK I...well I just thought I'd ask.'

I was embarrassed, my lies were painfully transparent and I knew that Dave must see through them. Why shouldn't I go? What did I have to lose? It was August Bank Holiday weekend that Dave was talking about, did I really want to be on my own over the whole holiday? I made a snap decision.

'Well on the other hand Dave, it might be fun and I could always do what I was planning another time.'

'Of course you could,' Dave's tone was bright and welcoming, it encouraged me to go further.

'I could bring my keyboards.'

'Why not?' Dave laughed. As I put the phone down after we'd made arrangements, I realized that this event was the first thing

I'd had to look forward to for two years.

As the first light of day broke over tent city I was lying in my damp sleeping bag counting my aches and pains. I was twenty eight years old and used to hotel beds and en suite facilities. I had camped in a tent once before but that had been in glorious sunny weather in the South of France. Here in the green belt just north of London, it had rained hard since we had arrived three days before. My vocabulary held insufficient adjectives to describe the horror of the communal wash facilities and the toilets were beyond anything I had ever imagined in my worst nightmares. This was definitely not the South of France and yet – I'd had a wonderful time.

For someone like me, brought up as a student in the seventies, and attending the pop festivals of the time, Greenbelt '83, a Christian pop festival, was a very strange experience. For a start, in spite of the bad weather and the ever present mud, everybody seemed to be happy. Wherever I looked I saw smiling faces. At first I had put this down to the usual explanation of the availability of mind exploding drugs at pop festivals. Yet, as I watched the young people carefully as they browsed the stalls, or watched the bands, or spent time by their tents I couldn't spot one joint being passed around or dubious small parcel changing hands. My highly trained Seventies nostrils couldn't pick up the tell tale sweet scent of hash smoke. I couldn't detect one set of glazed eyeballs or one staggering walk. As far as I could tell, and this was really incredible, there didn't seem to be any booze in the place either.

So why were all these people looking high? What were they on? Were they merely simpletons, all ten thousand of them, or was there something I was missing?

It was Bank Holiday Monday, the last day of the Festival, I poked my nose out of the tent, expecting more rain. I got a blue sky and sun, lots of it. I hadn't slept well that night, apart from the damp and discomfort, I'd been woken very early by an over zealous rendition of 'This is the day the Lord has made' by a camper van full of children. At breakfast, the early morning chorus was the sole topic of conversation.

'I know their youth leader,' said Dave, biting into his bacon sandwich, 'I had a sharing time with him a couple of days ago in one of the seminars.'

I didn't know what Dave meant by 'sharing time', but I liked the idea,

'I wouldn't mind sharing one of two things with that group right now,' I said pointedly.

My thoughts turned to questions of organization and management.

'Dave, I don't think I've seen any police around, where's the security?'

'Don't need many police, I think there's a couple around somewhere.'

This was even more unbelievable than the absence of drugs.

In spite of Dave's invitations I had studiously avoided attending any seminars. I didn't want to be lectured, besides I'd heard it all before. Part of my education had been at a Cathedral school where morning prayers were said every day in the Cathedral itself. I had been confirmed, aged twelve, in the same Cathedral by the bishop with my father and mother in attendance. I had sung in the local church choir, first as a soprano then as a tenor. Finally I had read theology and English literature at University. Something had attracted me to the church all those years, but I didn't know what. Nothing had seemed really real. Saying prayers in the morning was merely part of the daily ritual at school, being confirmed was just the thing you did at that school at that age. In the choir, I had sat through hundreds of sermons, but listened to very few. I knew the order of service and the litany off by heart, a natural result of having to recite it countless times as a choir member. Church, as far as I was concerned, had almost become a place of work, where you could also socialize and get a few laughs afterwards. It was a club like any other, only instead of going on fishing trips, or making model boats or collecting stamps you sang and you happened to sing in a church.

At university I had studied the Bible just as I would have studied any other historical document. I looked for flaws in the text, for discrepancies between texts and for ambiguity of meaning and found plenty. I was surprised, at first, to discover that several of my theology lecturers were atheists and made no secret of it. Initially I found this hard to understand, it seemed rather like asking a Nazi to lecture people on the riches of Judaism. As I studied more, however, I began to realize that you don't have to believe in something to be knowledgeable about it. I began to exchange the naivety of my earlier views for a more sophisticated standpoint and, in this case, sophisticated meant sceptical.

My scepticism had lasted from my university days to the present. I had still dabbled with faith, occasionally attending my local church whilst pursuing a career in teaching and making music. However recent events had more or less destroyed any remaining bits and pieces of belief I still had. As far as I was concerned no loving God would have allowed the total collapse of my life that had taken place over the last two years. One had only to look around at world events for proof that if there was a God, he was either on vacation or had a strange idea of love and mercy.

And yet for all that I still couldn't dismiss the real sense of caring and commitment I was witnessing at this annual get together of the nation's Christian youth.

If the seminars couldn't hold the answer for me, perhaps I would find it amongst the stalls offering various Christian related arts and crafts. I wandered for a couple of hours, enjoying the sunshine and the relaxed atmosphere that it brought. I was impressed with the number of organizations and charities working in the developing world. People were travelling to every corner of the planet under Christ's banner it seemed, but I knew that there were an equal number of organizations operating under other religious or humanist colors. I needed something unique, something which no other faith or organizational religion had, something real.

By late afternoon I was pleasantly exhausted. I'd walked around the entire site many times chatting with stall holders. I'd even bought a couple of items, a leather bible cover for Dave to say thank you for bringing me and another item for myself which I wasn't going to show Dave. In a corner of the festival village I'd come across a stall selling merchandise that I was sure the organizers wouldn't approve of. Amongst this dodgy selection I found a greeting card that said: 'Jesus Loves You – it's just everyone else who thinks you're a plonker'. This appealed to the politically incorrect side of my humour, I had swopped conspirational glances with the stall holder as I handed over my money, like two spies meeting in enemy territory.

As night fell everyone prepared for the final evening's entertainment. Dave's group had positioned themselves early right in the front of the mainstage. I was impressed with their advanced planning.

'I can see you've done this before,' I said laughing to Dave.

'Just once or twice,' came the reply. I was in a teasing mood.

'What I don't understand though is why you need to come here so early, surely with the amount of brotherly love in this place you could arrive last and somebody would make a space for you right at the front if you asked.'

Dave gave me a straight look.

'Well it's true to say that I love my brothers and sisters in Christ and I'd do anything for them.'

I prepared to respond, Dave beat me to it.

'Except, that is, give up my front center pitch in front of mainstage on the last night of Greenbelt.'

I soon found out why. The atmosphere was supercharged as band after band led the audience in wave after wave of 'hands in the air' praise of their God. I watched in amazement, church had never been like this, there was an unrehearsed rawness about it that was deeply moving. It seemed to me that people were jumping up and down and waving their arms in the air not because of chemical stimulation but because they were expressing how they felt about what they believed. Neither was it due, as the critics of such events often said, to group hysteria. The energy was already in the audience, long before the concert started, I had seen that by the way people had been behaving all weekend. This wasn't a false temporary high, the sort I had so often experienced myself at other concerts and which left you flat the next day. There was something lasting here, but what was the secret? I made a mental note to discuss these matters more fully with Dave as soon as I got a chance. Then something happened that I wasn't expecting, the lead singer, an American Gospel singer called Jessy Dixon, called for quiet and started speaking:

'If you're standing there tonight wondering what this is all about and wishing you knew, then this is for you. All you need to do is to open your heart and say this prayer with me.'

I braced myself, this was the embarrassing part. I had thoroughly enjoyed the music and wished they would skip this 'holier than thou' section. I had seen American evangelists do this kind of thing on TV and always cringed when I saw it. I hoped this part would pass quickly. Jessy started praying the Lord's prayer. I was surprised, surely this was a bit old hat for such a hip gathering, I had expected more fire and brimstone.

Then the strangest thing happened. As I stood in the middle of the crowd something told me that this prayer was for me. I had an inescapable certainty that this was all especially for me, a certainty that grew with every passing moment. I had heard the

Lord's prayer a thousand times, recited it a thousand times, but now I felt, for the first time, the power behind the words, the reality that had eluded me all my life.

I started repeating the words of the prayer quietly to myself, I had no idea what was happening. I felt a mixture of nervousness and elation as I prayed, I glanced at the others around me, Dave and his group were also praying, as I found out later not for themselves, but for me.

A warm summer breeze blew across the field in which the crowd stood, I looked up, it was still just light, the sky a deep lustrous blue, I started to weep.

There was nothing I could do to stop it, I wept openly and uncontrollably. As I wept I gradually became aware of a feeling of lightness, as if my body was becoming physically lighter. I knew that something was leaving me, something that had been with me for a long time. And there was another thing, something that was entirely fresh and new. For the very first time I had a sense of my own guilt, my own faults that had led to the break up of my marriage. I saw myself through Jill's eyes and listened, for the first time, to the things she had said to me in our final days. It was too late for us now but not too late for me to learn. I felt profound gratitude that I was being shown the truth, all of it, and that I was ready to accept it with humility I was both within myself and outside myself, watching what was happening from a distance, time stood still. I knew something amazing was happening to me, but I was no longer in control, there was another hand at the wheel.

Then, in that moment, I knew. This hand belonged to the Jesus of history, the Jesus I had studied and yet never really known. Now He was real and He was alive and He was standing beside me. I was overwhelmed, I dropped to my knees. I could still hear the words coming over the PA system

'...in the name of the Father and the Son.'

I felt other hands gradually lifting me, other voices gently speaking to me. It was the end of things and the beginning of things, the end of days and the beginning of days. I had gone to a festival organized just for me, attended a concert staged just for me and said a prayer prayed just for me. The stripping away of my old life that had started two years before had led me to this place and this night. God hadn't been able to reach me while I had surrounded myself with my comforts and my scepticism, I needed a simpler, younger heart.

There was to be no sleep that night, I lay awake for hours in my tent, it was if my whole body were on fire. I tried to analyze what had happened to me, but this experience defied analysis, you either accepted it or you didn't. Either way there was no doubting its reality.

In the morning at six o'clock the chorus of 'This is the day' started up again , the camper van full of children rocking from side to side. I laid in my sleeping bag and sang along with them, overcome with joy.

Blind

(words for ballad)
Can't sleep tonight
Too many songs in my mind,
going blind,
too many futures my eyes can't see.
Mists swirl around the streetlamps
each a lonely pool of light,
long cat cries,
calling and gargling along deserted streets.
Consecrated by love I write words
forged in fire
ablaze with passion and longing,
a light to lighten the
deserts of darkness all around,
And now, through my window,
the steel gray of dawn,
the light you brought to the world.
I have no words to give you except these,
rantings of a madman
half crazed ,
stuttering laughing shouting hoping stumbling my way,
from this sightless night
into blinding day.

Chapter 2: The Beginning (Part Two)

After such a dramatic conversion it seemed the only thing to do was to make a fresh start. Not being one to do things by halves I packed in my job teaching in a secondary school, sold my house and everything in it (what was left of it) and moved to Paris. This wasn't quite the irrational move it may seem at first. I had spent a year training to teach English as a foreign language in the evenings, the job I started was reasonably paid and, most importantly, offered fresh horizons where I hoped to put the past to rest once and for all.

Within a month or two I was a regular at the main English speaking Anglican church, St Michael's, within another month I was playing the piano and leading the music worship group at the Sunday services.

The church did a very good job at creating a home from home for young ex pats who found themselves in Paris, often alone and homesick. It's fair to say that maybe only fifty per cent of those who turned up on Sundays were actually Christians, the rest were looking for company of other young people who spoke their language. Such a person was Jane, she came from a troubled family background in Cornwall and had found herself a job as an au pair to escape. She was very young, only seventeen, but her experiences had made her old beyond her years, I had never met such a world weary seventeen year old before, more of her a little later.

I had soon settled into the Parisian lifestyle, doing my impersonation of a sardine in Le Metro every morning, on my way to teach English to wealthy French bankers. It was hard work and my time at St Michael's became very therapeutic, where I could relax and, above all, pursue my love of music with other musicians. These were students at the Conservatoire who were studying various string instruments to a very high level. Our music group was therefore pretty good and it was a delight to play with it every week.

It was against this background that the news broke that we were all off to a retreat for a long weekend at a Chateau outside Paris.

The church was bearing all expenses and the event was open to all, we were told that the guest speaker in residence for the weekend would be Gerald Coates. I must confess that this meant nothing to me at the time, and even if I had realized that Gerald was a well known evangelist and one of the founders of the house church movement in the UK, I would probably still have been blasé about it.

At St Michael's, because of its status as the official church of the English Embassy, we were used to the sight of the Ambassador joining us for worship, we had also received a couple of retired Archbishops of Canterbury over the past few months not to mention many well known speakers visiting from the UK, Gerald would be just one more 'celebrity' Christian.

The journey to Charbonnieres by coach set the tone for the weekend. Everyone was in high spirits, this was a great adventure, and even those of us who were old enough to know better were caught up in the frolics. The atmosphere on board resembled more a bunch of naughty schoolchildren looking for mischief than a group of young Christians off for a time of reflection and spiritual refreshment.

I was looking forward to the weekend immensely, mainly because I would be playing an important role in leading the music group, nearly all of whom had signed up for the trip. I had no real idea of what was planned for the weekend musically , or any other way for that matter. So I had armed myself with my trusty copy of Mission Praise, which had just been published on the back of Billy Graham's Mission England. I was assuming that we would be playing the usual selection of choruses with the occasional hymn thrown in. At this stage I had written very little original Christian material, I was happy to play other people's worship songs as I had no sense of being called to musical evangelism, the idea of starting my own band wasn't even a glint in my eye as yet.

I'm pretty sure that the first evening at Charbonnieres was not really in keeping with what the organizers had probably hoped for. The scene resembled more an American frat party than anything else, wine flowed freely, the new curate got tied up his room, booby traps were laid for unsuspecting maids and overexcited people spent most of the evening running up and down corridors and slamming doors. Into this chaos, unbeknown to us, our speaker and his wife had arrived late at night after a difficult and stormy sea crossing from the UK....their chances of sleep were, of course, zero, until finally people started to go to bed at about four in the morning.

Breakfast was served at eight after morning prayers at seven, suffice it to say that neither event was well attended. I had made a superhuman effort to rouse myself from slumber and arrived in the breakfast room just in time to see Jane, who hadn't been to bed at all, staring intently at a poached egg before rushing out of the room to keep an urgent appointment with the lavatory.

It was a very ramshackle and subdued group of people who assembled in the seminar room at nine for the first session to be taken by Gerald. Stephen, the very conservative curate, was not a happy bunny and read us the riot act about our behaviour. We all felt embarrassed and stupid and decided to make up for it by singing a rousing chorus of 'Majesty', there was no piano in the room so it fell to me to start us off. As we sang it started to become apparent that our speaker was running late. Four renditions of Majesty later one of the admin staff at the chateau stuck her head around the corner and delivered a message in her best English:

'"Ze speaker, Monsieur Coat, 'e is late because 'e 'as not yet waked up yet.'

This made us feel even worse, as we knew exactly why our esteemed guest had overslept. There was nothing for it but to slog our way through some more choruses as our feelings of guilt increased by the minute. We felt like naughty schoolchildren once more, waiting for the arrival of the headmaster who was going to give us all a good rollocking. I think we must have sung for about a good half hour before Gerald and his wife Anona finally arrived.

I have never before or since seen a face so devastated by lack of sleep as the one which Gerald Coates wore that morning. He looked like one of the American army volunteers who, back in the 50's took part in experiments in sleep deprivation. The first thing he said to us that morning confirmed his status as a genuine Christian...*he* apologized to *us* for being late, blaming his late arrival the previous night. At that moment the hearts of every reprobate in the room warmed to him.

There then followed a morning of teaching of astonishing power, inspirational, spirit filled and radical. Here was a man at the top of his game with the ability to tap freely into God's power in spite of his own physical state. By the time lunch arrived, the group of juvenile delinquents from the previous evening that had somewhat grudgingly sat down at the start of the session had been transformed into inspired and challenged young people, chattering excitedly about issues such as the future of the church and the meaning of discipleship. Even Jane, who normally, was the least enthusiastic and most sceptical member was joining in with the conversations.

That evening had been billed, rather mysteriously we thought, simply as a 'group encounter session'. There was a magnificent grand piano in the room, which I took full advantage of, playing my heart out as we sang choruses and hymns at the start of the session. Gerald asked us to stand in a circle and, standing in the center, began to pray for each one of us individually, standing in front of each person. These were uncharted waters for the majority of us, the nearest we had come to this level of intimacy before was a piece of cake and a nice cup of tea at one of the house groups that we all belonged to. What was happening now was personal and challenging, it was uncomfortable and way outside our safety zones and yet , by now, we trusted Gerald and took part it in it fully, that is until it got to Jane's turn.

As Gerald reached Jane he visibly recoiled for a moment, then, after composing himself, he reached out to touch her on the arm. As soon as he made contact she spat at him:

'Get your f****** hands off me, you f****** b******!'

It's difficult to convey the force of the shockwave that hit the group, Jane had always been the quiet one, the one at the back, the one with very little to say except the odd muttered comment and nobody had even heard her raise her voice let alone swear before now.

Jane launched herself at Gerald amid a storm of screamed expletives and almost succeeded in dragging him to the floor. I caught a glimpse of her face, she looked as if she wanted to kill him. One or two of us stepped forward to intervene before she succeeded, Gerald immediately called out to us:

'It's OK, it's OK, this sometimes happens.'

This sometimes happens? None of the group had the slightest idea what was going on, our quiet somewhat troubled friend had become a screaming banshee, she had become someone else and here was Gerald saying it was OK, how could it be OK? Gerald began praying for Jane, I began praying for *myself*, I was shaken and panicking, I looked round at the others and saw a collection of ashen faces, we were all thinking the same thing, our fun getaway have–a–lark weekend had turned into something much, much more serious and we weren't sure how to handle it.

Jane had calmed down a little, enough for me to actually listen to what Gerald was praying, he was praying for healing for Jane, for the spirit of confusion to come out of her and for the Holy Spirit to take control. Again I was seriously ruffled, this was like being in a scene from *The Exorcist* but for real and it was very disturbing indeed. In the midst of it all I couldn't help but notice that Gerald was cool, calm and collected, like this sort of thing happened every day. Maybe it did for him, I remember thinking to myself, but it certainly didn't for me.

Gerald took Jane into an adjoining room and left us to our own devices for a while. For a few moments there was a stunned silence at which point my Anglican musical training kicked in...what do you do if there is an embarrassing silence in a service? Play some music of course. I began playing without any music in front of me and after a few bars realized I was playing 'Bind us together Lord'...it was just what was required, as we needed to get comfort one from the other and we sang with real feeling. Gerald came back in at that point and explained that a spirit in Jane had been confronted by the Holy Spirit and rebelled before being driven out. Jane was resting now but she was alright and would be fine, we said a prayer for her and for ourselves and quietly and thoughtfully made our way to our rooms, there was much to ponder on and we weren't exactly in a party mood.

I spent a lot of time that night in contemplation. Up till now my experience of worship had been rather "nice", tidy services with good music, good quality preaching and "nice" people in the pews. What had happened to Jane reminded me of my own conversion experience a couple of years earlier and the raw power of the Spirit when it is unleashed to challenge, cleanse and change. I wanted to be able to channel that power to reach people who had no idea of the power of God. Suddenly playing choruses in a worship group in Sunday services was no longer enough. I wanted more cutting edge use of music that would grab people by the ears and make them listen.

The next morning at breakfast we could all see that something extraordinary had happened to Jane, she was relaxed, smiling and putting us at our ease. She found it difficult to put into words what had happened to her, all she could say over and over again was that she felt cleaner. She was to come back from that weekend a changed person, as we all would. Just before we left I searched out Gerald for a quiet word. I told him how I felt about wanting to be able to do something more radical in the world of religious music. His response was typically no nonsense:

'Well you'd better go and do something about it then Scott and don't forget to pray!'

I knew he was right but I still hadn't quite got a handle on my own reasons for wanting to do it. It took another year or ten to sort that out, but it was a beginning of an exciting journey.

Chapter 3: The Band in the China Shop

After my experience at Charbonnieres I might almost be forgiven for the over enthusiastic approach that followed...almost. The fact is that my born again experience, coupled with my new musical ambitions had produced a wannabe St Paul, Martin Luther, Billy Graham and Cliff Richard all rolled into one, but without any trace of the wisdom that those men had. I had returned from Paris and found Pam, whom I chatted up with the line:

'Would you like to come to my baptism?' Amazingly she did, annoyingly being converted herself and taking her turn for baptism at the service before me three months later! Yes in every respect I was the fully equipped twentieth century Christian: brand new Bible complete with exhaustive commentary; a subscription to a monthly set of Bible notes just in case I'd missed something in the Bible commentary; subscription to a Christian record label sending me new releases by Christian artists every month; a set of uplifting posters bearing Bible passages accompanied by pictures of waterfalls, mountains, fluffy animals and sunsets adorning practically every wall in the house; Jesus stickers on books; Jesus magnets on fridge; regular attendance at home group and any seminars being held in my area; regular attendance at church services (even when raining); a prayer topic list pinned on the kitchen wall so I could pray with my cornflakes each morning and a 'Jesus Loves You' sticker in my rear car window.

Dave the drummer, who had invited me to Greenbelt, also had a car sticker. His mother had bought a brand new Ford Escort so that Dave could drive her around; it was his pride and joy. This car had been supplied by a dealership called 'Quicks' which, as most dealerships do, fitted all its cars with a sticker in the rear window to advertize itself.

Dave's Christian sticker had fitted just right above it, thus drivers following Dave's car were faced with the message:

Jesus is Lord
Quicks for Ford

I felt this rhyming couplet had unfortunate theological implications, suggesting that Jesus was Lord of all *except* Ford cars, if you wanted one of those you had to go to Quicks, besides ...it sounded daft.

When I pointed this out to Dave he was, as usual unimpressed, he had obviously thought it through, he explained it to me as you would to a five year old:

'Look, the fact it rhymes is good, it means people will remember it, advertizers do it all the time, what about 'Beanz Meanz Heinz?''

I felt Dave had missed my point along the way but let it go, I was far too busy planning my Gospel assault on the unsuspecting people of Manchester.

I was already well versed in the basic evangelical technique of turning every conversation around to God, so a simple observation about a weather forecast of, say, showers with sunny spells would trigger the following reply:

'Yes, I believe so, but thank God that it's not all clouds eh? We've got a bit of sun to look forward to. It's rather like life isn't it? You know we can have lots of troubles in our lives but a bit of sunshine can really turn things around. That's a bit like what happened to me, have I ever told you how I became a Christian?' It was now time to put my masterplan, hatched in Paris, into action. To my ego obsessed mind it was clear that I was meant to use my musical gifts for God, what could be more obvious? What other reason could God have possibly had to organize my conversion?

So it was that I set out to form a Christian band, this would be the vehicle to bring the power of God to the needy, just as I had seen happen in Paris. My first port of call was Dave who thought it was a great idea providing he didn't have to carry any gear that might scratch his mum's Ford Escort. Fortunately Dave's drum set and my keyboards just about fitted in the van I had at the time and 'Full Support' was in business. I was quite pleased with this name as I had seen on many concert posters the phrase: 'Starring (name of the band) plus full support.' I concluded that by the simple wheeze of calling ourselves 'Full Support' we would get free publicity on a multitude of posters plus the phrase described the full support that we received from Jesus as Christians. Unfortunately this brilliant idea hit the skids a couple of months later when a national ad campaign for a new type of bra used the phrase as one of its selling points. I had thought we could soldier on with the name until the night we played at a local youth club and the Youth leader's introduction of:

'I want you to put your hands together for Full Support!' caused mass hilarity.

We needed a new name and fast. I had always liked Jesus' words recorded in John 8 v36

'If the Son sets you free you will be free indeed .'

It was certainly true in my own experience and I wanted it to be true for others as well…the key notion was 'Freedom' and that became the name of the band that stuck for the next twenty years. Mind you I always kept a sharp eye out for ad campaigns for other items of lingerie promising freedom of movement.

Over the next three years or so 'Freedom' evolved into a group of singers with me as the sole instrumentalist. I had taken the obvious course of looking to my own Anglican church to provide new members and five people had come forward. Things were relatively easy, we rehearsed in the church free of charge, I had my own keyboards and PA equipment from pre Christian days and transport was in people's own cars. Gigs were supplied by using our own local contacts, pubs we knew, clubs we'd visited, ministers who had links with the church and so on. As well as this the vicar encouraged us by inviting us to play at one the church services, this soon became a regular booking and progressed to the stage where we would lead worship. As we were all busy people, doing this in our spare time, very often our rehearsal time was shorter than we would have liked and so, to save time, we often shortened the prayer time at the end. This eventually became a quick run through the Lord's Prayer before packing up.

Nevertheless everything was going well, we were busy and enjoying ourselves, the pub gigs felt more like social outings than ministry and we had become respected members of the church ministry team.

Or so I thought.

The first sign of trouble came in the shape of a phone call from one of the band member's wives. She was unhappy that her husband was out so much and accused me of trying to control him, adding for good measure:

'You know he's not that bright Scott and you're taking advantage of that.'

I was stunned, as far as I was concerned this had come from out of the blue. But worse was to follow. It seemed that news of this phone call was soon all over the church grapevine and the flood gates were open. One of the church elders, an influential member of the Parochial Church Council, had a 'quiet word' with me the next Sunday. She told me that she had concerns about the role of the band in worship:

'Sometimes it feels like the Scott Fellows show,' she said, adding, 'You know of course Scott I say this in love.' I had been a churchgoer long enough by then to know that this phrase always accompanied the feel of sharp cold metal slipping between your ribs, alarm bells started to sound.

As the storm gathered pace 'Freedom' activities were put on hold. There was to be a special meeting of the Parochial Church

Council to discuss these matters.

Over the next couple of weeks my bible commentary earned its keep. I gathered verse after verse, passage after passage to justify my position. What I didn't know was that others were doing exactly the same thing. Thus on the appointed evening the two sides entered the room as Roman gladiators must have entered the arena, but instead of wielding swords and tridents we were armed to the teeth with Bible quotations. Behind the scenes the church gossip machinery had gone into overdrive, I soon realized that, against this backdrop, the band's position was untenable, it was time to move on.

Only one person stayed in the band when I left the church and he, like me was a relative newcomer, the others had been members for years and were not prepared to give up their investments of time and service.

I had lots of time to lick my wounds and reflect on what had happened. For a long time I was convinced that I was the wronged party, after all, didn't Jesus himself in Luke 4 v 24 say that 'a prophet is never accepted in his own country'? As time went on however I began to reflect on our rehearsals, our performances, the way we had made decisions about where we would play and saw one thing missing...prayer. Yes we had prayed alright; the kind of cursory prayer such as grace before dinner, which, to so many people, is paying lip service without any real meaning; but we had never *consulted* God, we had *informed* Him of our plans and asked Him to bless them. No wonder things went wrong; God had become tired of being taken for granted. To paraphrase a famous line from the movie *Dirty Dancing*,' Nobody puts God in the corner!'

We had charged ahead with our plans like the proverbial bull in the china shop, treading on people's feelings, completely blind to God's will for us. It's a measure of God's grace that we managed to achieve anything at all in those days, that He would still bless us until even He had had enough.

On top of this I was still a very young Christian and some of the issues I had been suffering from before my conversion had still not been fully dealt with. One of these was an over supply of ego; thinking back to when we had led services I realized to my horror that, to an observer it must indeed have looked like the Scott Fellows show. I was the only one playing an instrument, I was the one doing all the talking between songs and choruses, I was even the one, on some occasions, delivering the sermon. Nobody else had got a look in and worst of all, that included God.

After a year or so of reflection I felt God was ready to give me another go at getting it right. I advertized for band members in Christian bookshops and was rewarded with three new band members, all of whom had strong witnesses of their own and, crucially, understood the importance of prayer and putting God in the driver's seat. This also ensured that I wouldn't be allowed to do all the talking anymore which was just what was required. So began a far more productive phase for the band, this time with God firmly in charge, which enabled us to pick ourselves up when things went wrong (and they often did) and to continue to develop as disciples, because God taught us something from every situation, every person we came across. In the years that followed the band line up changed several times, members came and went, but I never made the mistake of including God out again.

Devil's Song

'Take a little longer,' that's what he always says to you,
'There'll be time tomorrow, you need more time to think it through.
Don't be so impatient to tell the world about Jesus
Someone else can do it
There's no need for such a fuss.'
'Move a little slower,' you hear a whisper in your ear
'Don't you overdo it, there'll always be another year.
I know He will come just like a thief in the night
But take a little longer
To get the timing just right.'

Chapter 4: Strangeways

To get into the chapel at HM Prison Manchester (much better known as Strangeways) was, I imagine, almost as difficult as escaping from the prison itself.

First, for security purposes, names and addresses of visitors together with any vehicle details had to be submitted a week in advance and vouched for by a member of staff (in this case the Chaplain). Then on the day itself visitors had to present themselves in a tight time window to be allowed entrance and present ID at the gate. Any equipment must be carried by hand from the vehicle compound to the chapel itself (after being checked)...a simple enough task you might think.

The problem was that Strangeways was, and still is, a huge Victorian pile full of narrow corridors, twisting metal spiral staircases and here's the bad bit, no lifts. I can't remember exactly how many flights of stairs we had to negotiate with our heavy speakers and amps but it was a lot. By the time we reached the chapel door, we were already knackered before playing a note.

Entrance to the chapel produced a kind of Tardis effect, a small nondescript metal door on a top corridor with nothing to mark it as any different from the hundreds of other small metal nondescript doors. As we struggled through with our gear however we suddenly found ourselves at the back of a very large chapel, looking down past row upon row of raked seating to the flat altar area below. A prison officer came in behind us as we took in the view; he waved a huge bunch of keys in the general direction of the altar.

'You can set your gear up there if you want, most of the others do.'

By the time of this gig Freedom consisted of five singers...three male and two female with me on the keyboards. We had played in pubs and churches but no prisons...it's fair to say that some of us, particularly the two nineteen year old girls, were a little nervous at the thought. When I contacted the Chaplain's office I was encouraged by the warm response I had received. Yes they would be delighted to have us there, how soon could we come?

Of course many other Christian groups and singers had gone before us; in fact some of the prisoners had probably heard more Christian music and were more knowledgeable about the current contemporary Christian music scene than we were. The Chaplain's usual practice, especially for first timers like us, was to let us loose on the remand lads. These were young men in their late teens and early twenties who were waiting for sentencing on remand for mainly petty crime and who were considered by the prison to be a low security risk or Category C as they were known. We were let nowhere near the Category A lifers for which we were very grateful, these men received 'specialist' input from experienced prison visitors and had no time for the likes of us.

Our allotted time was just 40 minutes playing, which allowed a further 20 minutes for the lads to be brought out of their cells at the start and led back at the end , total 'recreation time' a strict 60 minutes.

Perhaps it was nerves, perhaps because we were already exhausted, but it took us longer than usual to set up that day. We were right in the middle of plugging in and switching on when we were shocked to find about thirty lads being brought in by two officers in single file. This was a prison and, as we were discovering, it lacked the social niceties of churches where we would be asked politely if we were ready before an audience were allowed in. Our 40 minutes had started ticking as the two officers retreated to the back of the chapel and sat, arms folded, staring down at us .

One of the girls, Nichola, a young pretty blonde, completely flustered by trying to set up feet away from a line of eerily silent young men , brandished a plug in the air and said loudly, 'I don't know where to put my plug.'

A half murmured voice came from somewhere in the line, 'I know where I'd like to put mine!'

I looked at Nichola, she had gone a deep shade of crimson, I looked at where the voice had come from to see three lads sniggering together. I looked toward the officers for help, they remained motionless, arms folded, expressionless...as long as those lads stayed on their seats they weren't going to get involved, we were on our own.

I took the plug from Nichola and whispered to her not to worry, the sooner we got started the better I thought.

We started with a loud rocker, probably too loud, in an attempt to show these lads that we were "cool".

The Oblivion Shuffle
(Hard rock beat)
Take it easy baby, play down cool
Take in the scene, shoot some pool
Act like nothin's happenin'
Maybe nothin' will
Just tell another joke and drink your fill
Relax have a dance, get with the beat
It's the oblivion shuffle, shufflin' millions of feet
They got no opinions, they got no views
They're told what to think on the six o'clock news.

The pace was furious, much faster than we normally played, a result of adrenalin pumping in our veins as we danced and gyrated in front of the motionless line of seated youth. It was a surreal experience, normally people would clap along or at the very least tap their feet...but nothing, no matter how loud or how fast we played. This state of affairs went on for three songs, just as were finishing the third rocker to another round of tumultuous silence our host, one of the prison chaplains, appeared at the back of the chapel.

He hurried down the steps towards us full of apologies at not being there to introduce us, having had to deal with an emergency in another part of the prison. There must have been something in our expressions that gave him a signal, he turned his back on the line, facing me and asked in a low voice, 'How's it going?'

'A slow start,' I replied

'Right!' he said and turned back to the lads. Working his way along the line, bent forward he spoke to them in conspiratorial tones, there was much nodding of heads, finally he turned back towards us.

'Do please carry on!'

One more fast one I thought and then we'll give up.

As the beat kicked in we saw what we had been waiting for, feet start tapping, hands clapped along and at the end we received some genuine applause. We were on our way and by the time we finished, that long silent line had turned into a laughing joking group of young people just like any other.

After exactly forty minutes the two officers at the rear of the chapel stirred themselves and the remand group were led quickly out of the chapel, no time for chatting or even goodbyes, in the wink of an eye they had gone, leaving us feeling a little robbed. It was after concerts that we enjoyed the opportunity to talk to people, to get to know them a little and share with them. There was to be none of that at HM Prison Manchester, the timetable was god and any other god had to fit around it.

As we struggled on the return journey through the bowels of the prison with equipment that seemed twice as heavy as it had done on the way in I remember the group being pretty downhearted and I was asking myself if what we had done would make any difference at all.

It wasn't until nearly two weeks later that I got an answer to my question. Towards the end of the concert we had played a song called 'Always' which I had written especially for the visit, it was a slow gentle ballad in which I had tried to capture what I imagined some of the prisoners might be feeling and to include a message of hope.

Always
You know this world can be a cold cold place
It takes your hopes and throws them in your face
And sometimes you never get a chance to make a proper start
Sometimes life can break your heart.
And people always let you down
When you give your trust and you're left playing the clown
And so you get hard inside
There's nothing left to believe
And you get no place wearing your heart on your sleeve.
But ain't it good to know
When you've got no place left to go
That He still loves you when you're right out in the cold
No matter where you are
No matter what you are
No matter who you are
He loves you as you are…always
And so you pass on down the line
You find different ways to pass the time
But you're not sure what you're waiting for
When every way you turn someone closes a door
Sometimes there seems to be no end
Sometimes you're left without a single friend
And all the time you struggle on
You're scared to stop the fight
But much too tired to go on alone
But ain't it good to know
When you've got no place left to go
That He still loves you when you're right out in the cold

No matter where you are
No matter what you are
No matter who you are
He loves you as you are...always

We didn't know it at the time but those lyrics had found a home in at least one heart. A week or so later a letter arrived for me, forwarded by our chaplain friend from David, one of the lads we had sung to that day.

In the letter he told us that at the age of just twenty one he had been in and out of remand homes and prisons for as long as he could remember, mainly for petty crime. His parents were both committed Christians but he had always regarded them as a bit touched. Now things had changed dramatically; something, he wrote, had happened during our 'Always' song, something which he couldn't explain but he now knew that Jesus was real and he had, with the Chaplain's guidance, now made a firm commitment to the Lord. Here's a brief extract from his letter:

"...you made me realize that Christianity isn't just doom and gloom, which is what I thought it was...you helped recreate my faith in life and showed me how to be full of joy and peace and love. The lines that really spoke to me were in your song 'Always' which said that no matter who or what or where I am (even in this place!) God accepts me as I am I think that's great.'

As I read this letter I was tremendously moved, it was clear that the power of God had overcome every barrier that day. In fact, in years to come, that song would turn out to be easily the most popular of all our songs...I guess because its message is universal. We *all* need to feel loved and accepted *as we are* yet so many of us aren't, in fact it can quite often be the opposite. Jesus' simple message that God's love is available to all, which he demonstrated by some of the company he chose to keep that shocked the great and the good of his day, is tremendously powerful and can reach anybody, anytime, anywhere.

Perhaps the most important lesson I learned was that, as the old hymn says 'God is working his purpose out as year succeeds to year.' It was clear that David was meant to hear that song and the only place he would ever hear it was a place where he was required to sit and listen quietly to the lyrics...a place rather like a prison chapel in fact.

I was happy for David and at the same time deeply ashamed about my lack of faith in God. I realized that, though I had written in the song that God accepts us no matter what or who or where we are, I had signally failed to realize that this also went for God's ability to work.

He could, and did, work in the unlikeliest of settings with people who might seem far off and, here's the best bit, use the least of His servants to be His hands, His feet and His voice.

Mind you a little bit of persuasion doesn't go amiss either from time to time...the next time I spoke to the Chaplain I couldn't help asking what he had said to those lads that had produced such miraculous results.

'So come on Jim...what *did* you say to them?'

'Oh simple,' he chuckled, 'for recreation hour the lads are given a choice of board games or chapel...most of them choose chapel, not because they're particularly religious but because it gets them out of their cells for an hour with a chance of seeing a female or two, especially if they're good looking. I'd already primed them from the publicity photo you sent me.'

'So that's why we had such a good turn out, but what did you say to them?'

'I simply told them that if they didn't buck their ideas up I would ask you to leave and start a Bible study instead.'

We both laughed, the chaplain clearly understood exactly how to communicate with those lads.

Little did we realize that less than a year later another, much harder group of prisoners, would start the most serious prison riot in British penal history in that same chapel. When I heard the news I realized that not only had God reached out to David when we visited, He had also sent His angels to protect us, what a truly astonishing and gracious God He is.

Across the Waters

Like a forgotten army
Like a man without a soul
Like a waterless river
We need you to make us whole.
Like a child with no father
Like a bird tied to the ground
Like a man without a spirit
We were lost but now we're found.
Like a picture with no sunshine
Like a night without a day
Like a stranger with no guide
We need you to show the way.
Like a man caught in a tempest
On a dark and troubled sea
We need you to calm the waters
Join hands you sons and daughters
Stretch out across the waters
And the blind will see

Chapter 5: New Year's Eve at the 'All's Well'

It was coming toward the end of a long hard night at the 'All's Well' public house in one of the less salubrious suburbs of Manchester. The irony of the pub's name had not escaped us during the evening which had seen us provide the musical accompaniment to a couple of fist fights in the pool room and numerous loud and expletive filled verbal exchanges between various members of the clientele.

To be fair we shouldn't really have been surprised...the pub had a reputation for being dog rough and we had been warned in advance not to play it, it's just that we hadn't really realized just how rough some dogs could be. In fact some of the locals made a bunch of rottweillers look like a group of fluffy poodles playing gaily in the sunshine. The whole scene of extreme unpleasantness was presided over by Manchester's answer to Godzilla, Jackie, the 300 pound landlady manhandling offending customers single handed through the front door. On top of that it was New Year's Eve, the pub was packed out and a couple of the draught beers had already run out much to the disgust of the clientele...things weren't looking good.

We were playing in the lounge, which could be distinguished from the pool room by the absence of a pool table, slightly less spit on the carpets and not much else. It certainly had aspirations to be more upmarket, as evidenced by the cheery sign that greeted potential customers on the door:

NO DOGS
NO BOOTS
NO KNIVES
NO TRAVELLERS

Strangely, for a place so oblivious to equal opportunities issues the place was bristling with aids for the disabled. A ramp ran from street level up to the entrance, chairs and tables were spaced out so as to allow easy access for wheelchairs and there was a separate disabled toilet. I couldn't help wondering if all this was for the benefit of the customers who had once been on the wrong end of a snooker cue in the pool room and who now spent their convalescence in the lounge.

The time was about 10.30pm and although, in this era before twenty four hour licensing, the landlady had applied for an extended licence, old habits die hard so there had been the traditional mad rush to the bar with rows of pints being set up to tide them over until the time when they would be finally 'persuaded' to leave the premises by the "missing link" landlady and search out the nearest kebab shop.

In our experience this part of the evening was often the most fruitful in terms of speaking to people and sharing the Gospel. We took a break, got ourselves a drink and signalled for the jukebox to be switched back on. As we positioned ourselves strategically around the pub the jukebox cranked itself up and started blasting out 'Chirpy Chirpy Cheep Cheep' by Middle of the Road.

Although most people were too drunk to be bothered with anything but sitting and lapsing into a semi comatose state, the odd punter remained sufficiently aware to talk to, drink loosened their tongues and broke down their inhibitions about talking to a complete stranger. We often found that some people were ready to talk about things that really mattered to them, their relationships, their hopes and dreams in a way in which they wouldn't dream of doing sober and tonight was no exception.

I ended up sitting next to a man in his mid forties who was steadily working his way through three pints of Newcastle Brown that sat before him on the table. He eyeballed me as I sidled up alongside him. His opening line wasn't very encouraging:

'Did you stick this f****** s*** on?'

I denied responsibility for the appalling music on the jukebox, though took the opportunity to point out that Middle of the Road's later hit 'Tweedle Dee, Tweedle Dum' had been marginally better.

His next question was equally challenging:

'You're a Bible basher aren't you?'

I owned up to being a believer, drunk or not, I knew from experience that it was always best to be straight in these kind of conversations. I needn't have worried though, within minutes we were talking like two long lost pals...the drink had done its work.

It turned out that my new friend, John, had led a pretty miserable life, a drunk abusive father who left home when he was eight, a mother struggling to bring up him and five other children, bitter memories of poverty and the daily struggle.

The emotional damage done to him at an early age had resulted in an inability to interact properly with people...his own marriage had failed after three years resulting in divorce and losing touch with his daughter who, he told me, would be celebrating her sixteenth birthday in two days time.

This was a man who had never received the love he needed as he grew up and was never able to give it in later life. He was tired and emotional as we talked together, he spoke quickly, agitated as he recounted the various disappointments of his life finally trailing off as he became exhausted with the lateness of the hour, with the drink, with the memories.

I shared with him my own journey to Christ, the break up of my marriage and the healing brought about by finding Jesus. He listened intently, making eye contact with me for the first time, as if searching my features for the answers he was obviously looking for. He asked questions, lots of them, the kind of questions a child asks when they're learning about some aspect of the world for the first time.

We were so engrossed in our conversation that neither of us noticed the formidable shape of Jackie looming up on the horizon. She was staring at me intently.

'Have you run out of bleeding music or what?' she enquired.

I jumped to my feet with the sudden realization that we'd been talking for ages and it was now less that half hour to New Year, the other band members scurried back from the dark corners of the pub and we started playing again. I decided to try just one of our quieter songs with a gospel message before we launched into standard sing-along fare in the build up to midnight.

Unfortunately my little experiment had failed to take account of a group of gents with shaved heads and a wide variety of tattoos standing at the bar that I had been watching work their way methodically through rows of pints. They were shouting loudly to one another with much hilarity and back slapping making it virtually impossible for anybody else to hear the words of the song. I was miffed by this blatant affront to my artistry and decided to cut into the song with a request through the microphone, I could hardly hide the irritation in my voice: 'I wonder if the guys at the bar would mind toning it down a bit as some people are trying to listen to the music.'

This turned out to be a big mistake.

A sudden deadly hush fell over the pub, in fact it wasn't a complete silence as some people were still talking quietly, but in comparison with the deafening din of a few seconds before it certainly seemed like it. I looked at Jackie standing behind the bar, her expression of horror was total, she might just as well as been wearing a neon sign strapped to her forehead flashing out the word 'MORON!'

One of the group of drinkers detached himself and walked slowly over to us. Up to this point I had always thought this kind of scene was confined to Westerns from a bygone era, now I was being enlightened.

As my shaven friend got closer I could make out a couple of his tattoos, on his right forearm was a couple frozen in a compromising sexual position but, bizarrely on his left forearm was a red rose with the word 'Mother' underneath. I remember thinking at the time that here was a man with issues.

'Is there a problem pal?' To my surprise he was speaking quite softly, but this made it sound even more menacing.

'No, no, not at all, I was just wondering if you could tone it down a bit that was all.'

'Put it this way,' his tone had lowered to a near hiss, 'why don't *you* tone it down a bit.' He turned towards his associates at the bar and raised his voice, 'Cos we can't hear ourselves talk can we lads?'

This was met by a lot of histrionic nodding and 'yeahs' and 'too rights'.

He looked back towards me:

'You see the problem don't you?' there was no delay in my answer.

'Oh yes, of course.' He gave me a sneering grin:

'Good , well that's sorted then.' He called over once again to the gaggle at the bar:

'Our friend has kindly agreed to tone it down a bit. Mind you we might need a bit of brickwork later.'

The sneers from the bar wafted back to us:

'Thanks very much.' 'Cheers.'

I felt humiliated and threatened......brickwork? What was he talking about? I had visions of being accosted in the car park later I tried to push those thoughts to the back of my head. To my relief the gang of heavies decided at this point to drink up and leave. I felt much safer as I looked at my watch, it was 11.45pm, looking round the pub at the vast majority of punters who didn't know what day it was, let alone the time, I made a decision. I'd had enough and, after a hurried consultation with the others in the band, I switched my mike back on:

'Well ladies and gentlemen it's time to fill your glasses and join with us to count in the New Year.'

With hardly a pause I started counting down from ten to zero:

'….three, two, one Happy New Year!', followed by one chorus of Auld Lang Syne.

So it was, that in one rather grubby corner of Greater Manchester, 1984 arrived thirteen minutes before anywhere else in the UK.

We began to pack up, completely unnoticed by anyone in the pub who were now engaged in an orgy of kissing, hugging and mutual slobbering. Although we would be glad to get out of there in one piece this was, in a sense, also the hardest part of the whole evening, having to pack up and break contact with the people we had been talking to…I had learnt early on that this was the point at which trust in the Lord was all important. I couldn't control, for example, what would happen now to John, the seeds had been sown and now I had to walk away. There were lots of unanswered questions: Would what I said to him mean anything? Would he even recall meeting me the next morning? Would he ever follow up on our discussion and try and find out more about Jesus? I suppose in all the years of pub ministry we only got to find out the result of hundreds of similar conversations on a handful of occasions. This was in marked contrast to the kind of dramatic instant results often seen in large rallies or church services. Ours was a different kind of ministry in a very different setting and God usually chose to light a slow burning fuse under His Word. We learned in time to accept this but it did make the few times we did get to see the fruits of our work even more precious to us.

As I watched John take his leave and walk slowly and unsteadily to the door another punter crossed my line of sight blocking my view. I shifted to the right a little to continue watching John, so did the punter, I became aware that he wanted to speak to me as he swayed alarmingly. For one dreadful moment I thought my soft spoken, well shaved friend had returned for round two but as the face before me came into focus in the dim light I was relieved that it belonged to somebody else. His speech was slurred and heavily accented:

'You're one of t'band aren't ya?'

I owned up, the clue must have been the large keyboard I was now holding.

'You was enjoyin' yourself wasn't ya.'

'Yes, it's always good to come to the 'All's Well',' I lied

'Aye,' he paused to steady himself for a moment: 'Well I think you were crap!'

With that he pirouetted on one leg and began staggering to the exit, he paused for a moment and turned back toward me:

'Happy New Year!'

I permitted myself a sigh as he fell out of the swing doors, I continued packing up…as I struggled out of the pub carrying one of the very heavy speakers, I immediately noticed two things.

First it was raining, not lightly, not even moderately, but monsoon-like.

Second, through the wall of water, in the dim lights of the car park I could just make out our van, wheeless and sitting on four piles of bricks.

Now I knew what "brickwork" meant.

I Crucify

I crucify
Every time I live another lie
I crucify
When I see my brother and walk on by
I crucify
When I talk of others on the sly
I crucify
When I seem as sweet as apple pie
I crucify
While I judge another from on high
I crucify
I crucify my Lord again.
I crucify when I forget just why He died
I crucify
When the love He brought gets shoved aside
I crucify
When I lose myself in my own pride
I crucify
When I go to church just for show
I crucify
When I forgotten why I really go
I crucify
When I reap the corn but never sow
I crucify my Lord again.
I crucify
When I lock my mind and hide the key
I crucify
When I see the truth but let it be
I crucify
When the only one that counts is me
I crucify my Lord again.

Chapter 6: And Tonight Freedom will be Appearing With...

...Noel Proctor

Noel Proctor was for many years the chaplain of Strangeways Prison in Manchester. A diminutive Irishman nobly blessed as a preacher and evangelist. Many Christians had the experience of being inspired by his preaching, over many years. Noel is known for his story telling and his fondness for singing, and to this day, though now retired, is in enormous demand as a preacher and speaker

It was still the early days for Freedom and we were excited and thrilled when we were invited to provide the musical entertainment for a major outreach event which featured Noel Proctor as guest speaker.

When we pulled up outside the Central Methodist Hall in Manchester it was already evident just how many people were trying to get into the building. It would have been nice to think they were all there for us but of course it was Noel, as always, that was the big draw.

After setting up our gear and doing a brief sound check we were introduced to the man himself. I couldn't help smiling at the contrast between us as Noel shook my hand warmly. I was six feet four and 250 pounds, I estimated Noel couldn't have been much more that five feet four and was slenderly built. Noel wasn't slow to notice either

'Ah David and Goliath,' he said laughing, 'but don't worry I'm not going to slay anybody today.' He turned to one of the organizers, 'But I *could* murder a cup of tea before we get started.'

As somebody hurried off to get tea, I showed Noel the list of songs we were going to play before he spoke, they were nearly all our own material. He scrutinized the list closely:

'I don't think I know any of these.'

This was the moment I had worried about, many preachers liked familiar songs at their meetings and I wasn't sure if we would be able to play some of the songs that I knew Noel liked to sing.

'Well Noel it's our own stuff, but if you'd like us to play...'

'Excellent, excellent!' he interrupted, 'I'll look forward to hearing it.'

I was moved by his generosity of spirit to an unknown band like us.

We played our songs and the large audience, perhaps five hundred or so, were good to us and applauded warmly even though they must have been impatient for Noel to begin.

When he did begin, after the break, he was in top form, one minute reducing his audience to helpless laughter with one of his prison life anecdotes, the next telling moving stories of prisoners having their lives healed by Christ.

At the end of the meeting everybody adjourned to another large room where tea was being served. I spent some time lapping up the praise of people who had enjoyed the music. Eventually it dawned on me that I hadn't spotted Noel for a while, I wanted to leave but not before saying goodbye. With the help of one of the organizers I was led into the kitchen and there was Noel, literally up to his elbows in washing up, scrubbing furiously away and singing at the top of his voice. He never saw me, I backed out through the doorway and left quickly. I learnt an important lesson that day about Christian ministry and humility.

It would have been so simple for Noel to use his reputation to steamroller our choice of songs, so simple for him to leave the chores to others, after all he was the special guest and special guests don't do the washing up do they?

The fact was that Noel was prepared to live what he preached, if his Lord had been prepared to wash his disciples feet then why shouldn't he wash up some dishes? The mental picture of Noel covered in soap suds surrounded by stacks of dirty plates has stayed with me undiminished over the years. A picture, as they say, is worth a thousand words...or, in this case, a thousand sermons.

...Graham Kendrick

Graham Kendrick has been described as a 'father of modern worship music'. For more than 30 years he has been at the forefront of Christian music in the UK having written and recorded hundreds of songs, many of which are well known around the world. Graham is based in the UK and travels internationally participating in tours, festivals, conferences and training events, as a worship leader, speaker and performer.

In the early eighties when I was a very new Christian I became involved in a praise and worship event to be held at a meeting hall in Mossley, near Manchester. The worship was to be led by Graham Kendrick who at this time was just on the verge of becoming the universally known Christian musician and worship leader he is today. He needed a backing band, so Christian musicians from all around were invited to take part. Several rehearsals took place before the event itself and when the day came Graham showed up, totally professional, totally inspiring.

We completed our final run through at the end of which the organizer thanked us all and said that he had been praying for the success of the event which was designed to attract non-Christians.

Having some time to kill I was wandering around backstage when I spotted Graham through a glass pane in his dressing room door sat in a corner with his head in his hands. Now, although a wet behind the ears Christian I was no newcomer to the music scene in general and I knew stage fright when I saw it. I gently knocked on the door and, without waiting for a reply went in. Graham looked up, his eyes looked a little red I thought, I went into Good Samaritan mode.

'Don't worry Graham you sounded great, we all know our stuff so I'm sure it'll go well.' I put a reassuring hand on his shoulder. He continued to stare at me for a few moments, he looked slightly puzzled:

'Thanks – uh –'

'Scott'

'Thanks, Scott I appreciate it.'

I left his room quite pleased with myself.

Later on that day Graham did indeed lead a stunningly powerful worship session. Afterwards, when most of the audience had left, Graham came back into the hall to pick up his guitar, I seized my opportunity:

'You see! Nothing to worry about was there?' I gave him by best patronizing smile, he thought for a moment and then came over to me and put his arm around my shoulder, he spoke quietly:

'Scott isn't it?' I nodded

'Well Scott, what was going on there was me praying for the folks who will be coming to the evening. I always do that to prepare myself. I think you might have got the wrong end of the stick.' He smiled, the kind of smile normally reserved for very old confused people or sick animals. There wasn't a trace of sarcasm or unkindness in his voice, he was putting me straight as gently as he could.

As you can imagine, at that particular moment, I would have welcomed death as a friend.

...Bernard Manning

> *Bernard Manning was a Manchester born stand up comic. He
> became nationally well known in the UK through TV appearances
> on programmes such as 'The Comedians' and 'Wheeltappers and
> Shunters' in the 70's. He courted controversy throughout his career
> for his use of material which some found racist and offensive. His
> base was the club he inherited from his father, 'The Embassy' in
> Harpurhey, Manchester, where he appeared almost nightly for many
> years until his death in 2007.*

It's fair to say that Bernard's stand up routines were not noted for
their Gospel content. His club, the Embassy, was a place where
you checked in your conscience along with your coat at the door
and picked them up again on the way out .

I came across Bernard in 1983 just after becoming a Christian.
After the break up with my wife I had to find a fast way to make
some extra money. I'd done this by signing up to an entertainment agency, imaginatively titled Ace Agency, which was run
single handed by an enormous man called Doug who sat in the
living room of his council house, permanently shouting down
three phones at once, matching up keyboard players with clubs
who needed someone for the night.

Because I was a recent addition to his books, Doug only ever
gave me the dregs, the last minute stuff where one of his regulars
had fallen ill (or off the wagon) and he needed someone to cover.
He would always call between six and seven o'clock on a
Saturday night and we would have a brief conversation, which to
a casual bystander must have sounded like two spies talking in
code:

'Hi Doug.'
'Droylsden Football club. Free and Easy. Thirty notes.'
'Time.'
'Soon as...'

'Contact?'

'Ask for Walter.'

I had been doing this kind of stuff almost on a weekly basis for over a year before my conversion. After becoming a Christian I had started to become more and more uncomfortable about some of the places I was sent to and acts I was appearing alongside. The standard Saturday night in the clubs nearly always included a comedian (nearly always blue), a music act and a stripper, not exactly the kind of social life encouraged by my church.

I was on the point of deciding to give up this kind of work when one of Doug's regular Saturday calls caught my attention:

'Got a special treat for you tonight Scott. Dots. Embassy Club. Sixty notes.'

This was big money in 1983 , 'Dots' meant I would be sight reading music provided by a singer. It appeared that the resident keyboard player had fallen suddenly ill after his face had had an unexpected meeting with the clenched fist of his girlfriend's husband, so I was on. The Embassy Club was a much bigger venue than I was used to but I wasn't too phased simply because I had met the owner, Bernard Manning, before. I had worked previously with his niece Francesca on a music project and as a result, at the start of the year I had paid a courtesy visit to 'Uncle Bernard' at his home. A visit where your host spends the whole time dressed only in Y fronts and string vest is not one you forget in a hurry. I was aware of Bernard's reputation as a racist but on this one and only visit to his home I found him friendly and easy going, perfectly normal in fact, save, as I said, for the bizarre dress code.

On my way to the club that night a plan was beginning to form in my mind. Here was a great opportunity to sing and witness to hundreds of people who, in my view, really needed saving. I decided to ask Bernard for a brief ten minute slot so I could sing one or two Christian songs between 'turns.' Strictly speaking this wasn't a 'Freedom' gig as the band didn't exist at this time, I was solo, but that wasn't going to stop me.

I arrived with only a few minutes to spare before the first act was on stage, as I entered the dressing room, the singer, Tony Cortez, shoved some music into my hands and started talking me through how many repeats he wanted, the tempo and so on. I was eager to get to Bernard who was front of stage near the bar, this would mean breaking the rule that artistes didn't go front of house before or during a performance...but I was a man on a mission. God's work was to be done. Still holding the music I'd been given I walked down the corridor at the side of the stage and went out into the club in search of Bernard.

I found him deep in conversation with a couple of other men at the bar and so waited patiently for some time to speak to him, I noticed to my surprise that there was no sign of a drink, I found out later that, far from being a heavy drinker he was diabetic and teetotal, another Manning myth exploded.

The warm up comedian started his act. At last the conversation broke up, now was my chance:

'Bernard, Bernard...do you remember me? I came to your house once.'

He looked at me briefly, or rather *through* me.

'Did you?'

My bubble started to deflate.

'Yes, I'm playing keys for you tonight and I was wondering if it would be OK to do a couple of my own numbers...'

Just then the barman brought a phone from behind the bar:

'Call for you Bernard.'

I waited again, another long wait. The comedian finished.

Bernard finished the call and looked back at me, he'd obviously forgotten what I'd said, I started again:

'I was wondering if it would be OK to play a couple of my own numbers tonight, like I did with Francesca in the studio.'

The look on his face told me that he really didn't remember me and had no clue what I was talking about. I was determined to get through so drew a breath to begin again, just then I heard my name, the MC was calling me from the stage;

'We'll be able to bring on our next act ladies and gentlemen just as soon as we can find where the f****** keyboard player has got to.'

Blind panic overtook me, I'd missed my cue, the unforgiveable sin. I scrambled backstage watched by hundreds of pairs of eyes, as I joined the drummer he greeted me:

'Nice of you to bleedin' join us.'

Worse was to follow, because of my haste to get to Bernard I had neglected my usual set up routine and had failed to check the settings on my keyboard. As a result I began playing the first song, 'If' by Bread, three semitones too high. Those who know this song will know that it reaches a climax on a very high note. I realized early on that I was in the wrong key but there was nothing I could do about it as correcting half way through the song would have sounded horrendous. Now I knew what the helmsman on the Titanic felt like as he frantically tried in vain to avoid the huge iceberg looming up before him, he knew it was coming but was powerless to avoid it. As I listened to Tony yodel his way up to the final excruciating top note I knew I was in even bigger trouble than Tony's groin.

Needless to say no Gospel was preached that night and I had my money chopped in half for 'crap playing and being generally crap' as the concert secretary wittily summed it up. I never met Bernard again after that disaster and strangely was never asked back to play at his club. I had given a lousy witness, the only saving grace, if you can call it that, was that nobody there knew I was a Christian.

I knew however and for a long time afterwards was angry with myself for mucking up such an opportunity. It was much later that it occurred to me that maybe God didn't want me to witness that night, I hadn't prayed about it and had decided myself that it would be a good idea. Yet I was a brand new Christian with still so much to learn, I wasn't ready, though I thought I was.

Bernard has now moved on to crack his gags in a much, much bigger club. My night at the 'Embassy' taught me one important lesson that Bernard already knew very well...don't think about getting up in front of people unless you've got something to offer and you've put some preparation into it. It must be said that, in that respect, Bernard Manning was way ahead of some church ministers I came across in later travels.

...Ian White

Ian founded his Christian music label Little Misty Music in 1985 and through releasing a series of recordings, setting the Psalms to music, has become one of Scotland's best known Christian artists. He played at Mission Scotland rallies in 1991 and more recently has been heavily involved in charity work for India. His song 'The Cross is still there' remains one of the simplest yet most beautiful testimonies to the call of Jesus.

Ian came to play at a concert to be held at my church in the early 90s. I had persuaded my minister that organizing a series of evening concerts with well know Christian artists would be a good way of putting our church on the map and perhaps increasing our membership. This was partly the reason for my enthusiasm, however if I am honest, I also saw this as an opportunity to boost 'Freedom's' profile by tagging along with a well known name. As I put the evening together I made sure that there would be no other support artists except 'Freedom' and that we would get at least forty five minutes at the start of the planned two hour evening. I still didn't quite understand that the concert was supposed to be all about Jesus rather than the people up on the stage.

When Ian arrived on the day of the concert he had driven solo from Perth a very long drive and was tired, in spite of this he was keen to make a success of the evening and spent some time checking the sound and tuning his guitar. We had a chance to chat while this went on and soon I felt as if I had known him for years...he had that ability that all good ministers have of giving you the feeling that he was genuinely interested in you and what you had to say. When I showed him the running order...Freedom forty five minutes, Ian twenty minutes...fifteen minute break...Ian forty minutes...he raised no objections, though he must have realized that this unknown local band 'Freedom' would be getting almost as much stage time as him.

When a large audience turned up I was delighted, I remember saying to the other band members something really clichéd like: 'This is the beginning of something big folks!' This turned out to have about the same prophetic insight as David Steel's infamous exhortation to the British Liberal Party conference of 1981 to 'go back to your constituencies and prepare for government'. Oblivious to all else however, I was determined to showcase 'Freedom' as much as I could.

As we kicked off the concert, with Ian waiting in the wings, we were given the kind of polite welcoming applause that audiences give acts that they haven't come to see but whom they realize they have to put up with to get to the main act. Unfortunately I confused this politeness for genuine enthusiasm, we were playing our best stuff and, perhaps in another setting, we would have had an audience genuinely behind us. Here, however, people had paid good money to see Ian White and, as we soldiered on through our overlong set, the fidgeting started. By the time I was finally ready to relinquish the microphone a full hour had passed and it was supposed to be time for the interval.

Ian came on stage to warm applause and told the audience that he would play just one song now and a full set after the break, rather than make the first part overlong. There was no hint of criticism in his words but backstage the penny finally dropped. I had hogged the limelight, deluded that people had come as much to see us as Ian, I felt dreadful.

Ian went on to give one of the most Spirit filled performance I have ever seen in over twenty years of Christian music performance, finishing off with a new song 'The Cross is still there'. As for me, I couldn't believe that I could be just as misguided and full of myself as I had been with Graham Kendrick a few years before...had I learnt nothing? As Ian packed up at the end of the evening I wanted to apologize but felt too embarrassed. To my amazement Ian was full of praise for our performance and started to talk about mentoring me, with a possibility of visiting his studios in Scotland. I was overwhelmed with his generosity and excited at the possibility.

We kept in touch for a while after that evening, but Ian was a very busy man and eventually just couldn't fit me in to his frantic schedule anymore.

I genuinely didn't mind, he had offered me something far more valuable than a recording session, a real insight into how to put Christian teaching into practice, how to live it as well as preach it.

It was indeed, as I had said at the concert, the start of something big, but something quite different from what I had thought at the time. I was beginning at last to learn how to draw a horizontal line through the great god 'I' to form the Cross of Jesus, the Cross that, as Ian had sung, is still there and the Cross that saves us from ourselves.

...Stuart Ferguson

Stuart Ferguson is a Methodist Local preacher who works in the Tameside area of Greater Manchester, he is an author and raconteur and is in much demand for after dinner speaking.

Now, compared to the other illustrious names in this section, Stuart is in a lesser league in terms of celebrity status, that is, of course, unless you live in Tameside, an area of Greater Manchester.

Every now and then in our travels across the North we came across someone who stood out from the crowd, in a nice way that is. Such a man was Stuart Ferguson. To form a mental picture of Stuart you need to imagine Robbie Coltrane as Hagrid in the Harry Potter movies talking like Arkwright in 'Open All Hours' minus the stammer. If you don't know these references I encourage you to look them up as imagining a combination of the two in one person will certainly be an enriching experience.

For me, having only lived in the north for thirty six years and therefore still considered an imposter by the indigenous population, Stuart represented the stereotypical northerner. He still used words like 'ha'porth' (*translation: halfpenny worth = not much ... as in ' I don't give a ha'porth for your chances of finishing that meat pie...shall I help you?'* expressions like 'happen it will' (*translation: maybe it will ... as in 'happen it'll rain today happen it won't')* called a spade a shovel, had never been abroad 'Why would I want to do that?' and had no time for anything other than plain northern food (*for our American cousins this means every variation possible on the pie theme always served with chips (fries) gravy(brown meat sauce)and mushy peas (don't ask).* On one notable occasion, the wedding of my singing partner at the time, Nigerian born Dorike, I found Stuart and his wife sitting forlornly in a corner when everyone else was tucking into banga soup, groundnut stew and moi-moi. My enquiry as to the problem brought the gruff response, 'There's nowt to eat.'

If 'northerness' is a virtue then Stuart is due for papal beatification anytime now.

Another of his talents, apart from being northern, is to be found in the funeral department. Stuart was without doubt the busiest officiating minister at funerals in the Tameside area. Five or six ceremonies a day was not unknown and to each he brought his own brand of humor and sensitivity that eased the pain of the mourners.

Stuart was, and is, a very funny man, able to write and perform material which never failed to amuse an audience. When we first met Stuart we realized that with his stand up and our music, we could make a great team. So it was that for several years in the late 90s we performed together at concerts across Manchester and beyond. Stuart brought sketches and monologues, we brought our music and the audiences loved it. It was one of the happiest periods in the history of the band and it confirmed what I had always suspected: that humor breaks down barriers and conveys messages better than almost anything else. I can't help believing that Jesus must have had a smile on his face when he outwitted the scribes and the Pharisees with His 'Render unto Caesar that which is Caesar's and unto God that which is God's.'

If there's one reason that some churches are almost empty it's surely because they take themselves too seriously, people love to smile and if church is a 'smile free zone' as it too often is, then they'll vote with their feet. I often laughed out loud with the audience at some of Stuart's monologues which took a wry look at some aspects church life and gently poked fun at them. One example was a sideways look at churches suffering from a preoccupation with jumble sales. Here's a much abridged taster, which Stuart would deliver deadpan in the style of giving out the notices during a service, each individual notice was mildly amusing but the cumulative effect on a live audience well versed in the world of jumble sales was very funny indeed:

Jumble Sale Notices

On Saturday 6th, the Sunday school has their Anniversary Jumble Sale at 10am – at which extra biscuits will be served.

Next Sunday after Worship at 11am, Mrs. Ramsden has given me a note to say she wants a 'brief but vital' meeting with her Jumble Sale Group.

*On Wednesday 10th at 6.30pm the Rose Queen Mum's are holding an **Invitation only** Jumble Sale. This is to help boost their funds and 2,000 invitations have gone out door-to-door.*

*Now, on Thursday 11th we have a problem – but it's been sorted. At 6pm the Men's Fellowship were having a Jumble Sale, but we realized, after the advert had gone to the local paper, that we'd already booked the Hall for the Bowling Club Jumble Sale at 6.30pm. So the Men's Fellowship has kindly agreed to use Rooms 3 and 4 with the partition removed. So we've **two** Jumble Sales that night. Come in through the main doors for the Men's Fellowship Jumble Sale at 6pm and through the doors on West Street to get to the Bowling Club Jumble Sale at 6.30pm. We think that's fair to both groups. Unfortunately Walter Smith saw fit to hand in his resignation as Jumble Sale Secretary of the Bowling Club – but that's his problem.*

On Sunday 14th we have a special preacher, The Rev Ivory Collar, and his subject will be 'Evangelism through the Jumble Sale' so do come and hear this well versed man of the cloth.

Now on Tuesday 16th there's a Churches Together Jumble Sale – and that's held here at 6.12pm. That was a committee decision. They added up the starting times of the Roman Catholic, Anglican, And Congregational, United Reformed, Salvation Army, Methodist and Baptist Jumble Sales and averaged it out. So 6.12 it is. Well actually it came to 6.12 and 17 seconds but as it takes the caretaker 17 seconds to open the building we kept it to the nearest round figure. That's a time that's fair to everyone – and nobody likes it. Admission is 22 and a third pence.

On Wednesday 17th at 6pm we're holding a Jumble Sale to raise money to repair the roof of the Jumble Sale storage room.

On Friday 19th at 7pm is a Jumble Sale run by the young Wives. Senior Citizens Section.

On Sunday 21st it's our monthly Quiet Time Service at 9.30am in the Vestry. This gives us a chance to reflect on the Jumble Sales of the past week and to ask God to give us strength for the Jumble Sales that are to come.

In the afternoon the Women's Auxiliary Section have a meeting at 2.30pm with an illustrated Slide Lecture entitled 'Jumble Sales Over the Years'. All are welcome.

Now on Monday 22nd at 7pm we're invited to go to the local Synagogue for their Presidential Lecture on the history of Jewish Jumble Sales. Rabbi Kohl will talk on the 'Last Remnant of Israel' – and how much they got for it.

On Thursday 25th we're trying something a little bit different: A Good As New Sale. That's at 6 o'clock – and at 6.45pm we're having a Jumble Sale to sell the items that didn't go at the Good As New.

On Saturday morning, the 27th, at 10.30 am, we're holding out Jumble Table Top Sale in the car park. If it rains, forget it.

Stuart also became a great help to us in the never ending quest to get publicity out to churches and pubs. He and his wife Lynn spent hours stuffing envelopes, licking stamps and posting out letters on our behalf, just the kind of unglamorous work that any ministry needs behind it.

Stuart was a good friend to the band when we needed one and, though unknown outside his local area, didn't need to be, as he had absolutely no intention of going anywhere where you can't get gravy on your chips.

Chapter 7: Just a Song at Twilight

I had a bad feeling about this, a rock band playing in a care home for the elderly? It just wasn't right, but the care home manager had been very persuasive on the phone and hadn't hesitated to use emotional blackmail when I shared my misgivings:

'Well of course I quite understand if you don't want to do it, it's just that we've been let down at short notice by a ten pin bowling ball juggler, the folk here are desperately disappointed and when somebody told me about you I felt you would be an appropriate replacement.'

I privately resolved to find out who had passed on the information and have a quiet word with them.

To my amazement I then heard myself saying:

'Ah well we can't let our senior folks down can we? What are the details?'

I passed on the news to the rest of the band by phone, with, it must be said, a wide range of reactions. Dave the Drummer dispensed with the niceties:

'Are you crazy? Have you gone stark raving mad?'

'Look on it as a challenge Dave, something different, something outside your comfort zone.'

Dave wasn't impressed:

'Yeah, well a hot spike is different from a comfy chair but that doesn't mean it's a good idea to sit on it does it?'

Dave could be just plain awkward sometimes.

At our next rehearsals everyone had brought, at my suggestion, some secular music from a bygone era that we could mix in with our own stuff. All the usual suspects were there, songs warbled at various times by Frank Sinatra, Vera Lynn, Perry Como and the rest of the easy listening crowd. I think the most modern, edgy song anybody had brought was 'Little White Bull' by Tommy Steele. Neil the guitarist had dug out an old music book that had belonged to his uncle which contained such classics as 'It's a long way to Tipperary' and 'Down at the old Bull and Bush'.

I was getting fed up:

'Just how old do you think these people are Neil? They'd have to be over a hundred years old to remember this stuff when it came out, and look at this!' I'd turned over to a song called 'My Grandfather's Clock'. I jabbed my finger at the last line of the chorus and held it under Neil's nose as I read aloud:

'*It stopped short, never to go again when the old man died*...that'll go down a storm that will!'

By the end of the rehearsal and after, as political spin doctors call it, a 'full and frank exchange of views', we finally managed to agree on a group of songs that were post World War I and didn't mention death. By this time I was already regretting that I'd ever agreed to do the gig but didn't have the bottle to phone up and pull out. I'd gone through all the possible excuses in my mind...Van broken down, one of the band contracted typhoid, been called up for Jury service, grandmother on death bed...but I knew the manager wouldn't buy them, after all he was a bit of a wily fox himself, I wouldn't be able to outsmart him.

So it was on a cold Sunday afternoon that we pulled up outside the Sunshine Retirement Home. I was met by a woman with mop and overalls who was swabbing the entrance lobby floor. I attempted to be cheery:

'Working on a Sunday eh? Now there's real commitment for you.'

The reply was dead pan:

'One of our ladies has had a bit of an accident. Can I help you?'

I didn't get a chance to reply as the manager, Mr. Ellison emerged from an office nearby:

'Scott! Stuart Ellison, pleased to meet you.' He proffered a hand. 'Let me show you where you'll be playing.'

We were ushered into a large, bare room, populated by about thirty or so elderly octogenarians sitting on chairs arranged in a horseshoe shape around the perimeter. On the wall, surveying the scene, was an enormous picture of a smiling Queen Mother, probably grateful that she wasn't in there herself. It was a pretty grim scene; I noticed that there were no men,

'Where are the men?' I asked

Mr. Ellison lowered his tone to a near whisper,

'Unfortunately most men don't live long enough to make it in here. We only have one gentleman at the moment, Mr. Coates and he's in his room.'

'Is he poorly?'

'No he's fine; he just didn't want to come when he heard about you.'

Stuart gave me an apologetic smile; it didn't help the mounting feeling of alarm I was experiencing.

We started to bring in the gear, a route which took us past the staff room. Obviously working in a place where most people are hard of hearing had accustomed the staff to talk in constantly raised voices, even to each other. This meant that we were treated to extracts from their conversation as we hauled equipment to and fro. It was good to hear that our presence was already bringing about instant conversions, as one overheard conversation suggested:

'Who are this lot then?'

'A Christian group.'

'Oh Christ!'

We were just finishing setting up when I noticed one frail looking old lady beckoning me over to her, as I approached she engaged me in polite conversation:

'Mr. Ellison says that you're Christians.'

'That's right.'

'That's nice, do you go to church?'

'Yes I do.'

'That's lovely, do you say your prayers?'

'Oh yes every day.'

'That's nice, do you read your Bible?'

'Oh yes, as often as I can.'

'That's lovely.'

I could see this going on for hours, so thought I'd counter with a question of my own.

'Do you read your Bible?'

The old lady looked horrified:

'Oh no I've got no time for all that.'

I smiled and did a tactical retreat back to my keyboards, I had a feeling that this gig was going to be tougher than the 'All's Well' pub on a Saturday night.

Stuart walked to the middle of the room and spoke to the ladies very slowly and loudly:

'Now in a minute we're going to have some music from our visitors but before we get started is there anyone who needs toileting.'

A forest of hands went up and, as if from nowhere, an army of care assistants moved in to help people out of their chairs and to the toilets. In an instant our audience had dwindled to just six.

I turned to Stuart and, waving my hand in the direction of the remaining six, said jokingly:

'Well at least some of them have got strong bladders.'

He gave me a weary look:

'Not really, they're the ones with catheters.'

The whole process of 'toileting' took twenty minutes or so, which gave me ample time to work my feelings of regret up to fever pitch, by the time everyone had returned I was almost shouting my introduction:

'Good afternoon ladies.' I gestured to the band: 'We are called Freedom and we've come here to play for you this afternoon and to tell you about what we believe.'

One old lady in a wheelchair put up her hand, I paused and

looked at her hoping that I was going to get a question about faith. I should have known better:

'Are you any good?'

Another old dear next to her burst out laughing, a kind of high pitched cackle that reminded me of the Wicked Witch of the West in 'The Wizard of Oz', I attempted a witty riposte:

'Well that's for you to decide isn't it?'

Obviously my witty banter wasn't to her taste, she stared at me for a moment and then shouted to the back of the room,

'Jane! Jane! I want to go to my room.'

As she was wheeled out I couldn't help thinking to myself:

'One down, twenty nine to go.'

I suppose that, all things considered, the concert didn't go that badly. We worked our way through a carefully selected line up of easy listening songs and, as for our own stuff, kept well clear of the hard rockers. There was only one slight glitch when one lady started looking a bit uncomfortable, I thought I'd catch on to the routine and asked her:

'Are you alright? Do you need toileting?'

This suggestion was quickly repulsed;

'No dear, I've just got an itch I can't reach.'

I'd learned enough by now not to explore further.

To our immense relief we reached the last song in one piece and invited everyone to sing along with:

'We'll meet again'.

All went swimmingly until one lady burst into tears and needed comforting by her neighbours. Of course we felt dreadful but had to continue, never had a song seemed so long to me.

Stuart once again walked into the center of the room and did his impression of a Sergeant Major:

'Did you enjoy that?'

Wisely he didn't wait for an answer but pressed on quickly, I was beginning to realize I was in the presence of a master:

'I know *I* did and I'm sure we *all* did. Let's give Freedom a big round of applause.'

He came up to me as we began to pack up:

'Well that went pretty well didn't it?'

I hesitated for a moment:

'Well if you say so Stuart, I don't think we were really their cup of tea.'

Stuart gave me a wry smile:

'Look, we started with thirty and we finished with twenty nine...believe me that's an achievement in itself and it gave our ladies something to think about, that's good enough for me.'

We were joined by one of the assistants, she looked at me with a rather odd expression on her face:

'Excuse me but Mrs. Forbes would like to speak to you.'

I looked at Stuart, he clocked the look of alarm on my face:

'Nothing to worry about, Mrs. Forbes is very communicative, she enjoys a good chat.'

I approached Mrs. Forbes cautiously but soon started to relax as we started up a good conversation, she was indeed chatty and interested in the band. She was quite sharp and 'with it' as she spoke, not as eccentric or confused as some of the others, I was relieved. She wanted to know about whether or not we had ever worked with anybody famous:

'Well yes but you may not have heard of them because they're mainly famous in the Christian world.'

'Oh I see,' she smiled, 'you're probably right because I rarely manage to get out of here and I don't watch the television much except when certain people are on that I like.' She was giving me a very straight look as if she was weighing me up. She continued:

'Yes, thank God that I do have someone on the outside who thinks the world of me and I think the world of them. In years gone by we had a very *close* relationship.'

She emphasized the word *close* as once again she eyed me up.

'That's nice,' I said

'The problem is that he's so busy that we don't get to see each other, se we just have to write, I write to him every day.'

'Do you? That must take up a lot of your time.'

'Oh no no, I don't think of it that way, it's not a chore it's a pleasure, when two people are as *close* as us (once again the emphasis on *close*) then time becomes meaningless.'

'Well you certainly are a lucky lady to have that special person in your life,' I was beginning to feel mildly uncomfortable but didn't know why.

She latched on to my words with gusto:

'You're right! You're absolutely right, but unfortunately there is one problem.'

'Oh…what's that?'

Her tone went much darker:

'I have to share him, I don't have him to myself.'

'Careful now Scott,' I thought to myself.

'You mean…he's married?'

She almost spat out her one word answer:

'Yes.'

'Ah.'

'But I know he loves me and he doesn't love her.'

By now I was asking myself if this was a conversation I should really be pursuing. I decided to try and extricate myself.

'Well it's been good to meet you,' I stood up as if to go, Mrs. Forbes quickly grabbed my arm.

'Just a minute! Just a minute! You can do me a favour…would you post this letter for me? It's today's letter to him, normally I give it to the staff but you won't mind will you?'

She reached into her handbag and produced a pink envelope covered in hearts and kisses and handed it to me, I looked at the address, there was no address or stamp, there was just a name written in large capitals: BOB MONKHOUSE ,(*the famous UK comedian*). In the corner was written 'Private and Personal' and on the back S.W.A.L.K

I looked at the envelope and looked back at Mrs. Forbes, she was smiling sweetly at me and in that instant I knew that Mrs. Forbes didn't live in the same time-space continuum as me. I went off to find Stuart, clutching the letter, he was very matter of fact:

'Yes, Mrs. Forbes has been writing those letters since the day she moved in here which is over 5 years ago now and she was probably writing them before that as well, we keep them until her son visits and he takes them away. I don't know what he does with them.'

Mrs. Forbes confusion was complete, it was sad that this old lady had been overtaken by dementia in her final years and most likely very upsetting for her children to see her this way. The irony of course was that the only person who wasn't troubled by her condition at all was Mrs. Forbes herself who was far too busy plotting against her imaginary love rival...Mrs. Monkhouse.

Our visit to the Sunshine Home for the Elderly had been quite an experience. It had not been a success because we had pretended to be something we were not, a retro band specialising in the swing favourites of the forties and fifties. The importance of being real and honest with people was amply demonstrated by our failed gig that day, it was a simple lesson but one which had up to that point passed us by: If we wanted to bring people the truth about life then first we had to be true to ourselves and true to them. In future we stuck to what we knew we could do best, to give of our best to God who in turn was prepared to bless it...and if we ever came across a band that was due to play in an old people's home we always said an extra prayer for them.

OUR STAN

(up temp trad jazz to be sung in a Yorkshire accent)
Well let me sing the story of our Stan
And the way he lived and died
He was a grand old feller, you won't find none better
He never christened, swore or lied,
Well you'd find him alright, every Friday night,
Down at the pub with his favourite pint
He'd have a laugh and a joke, perhaps a quiet smoke,
A better man you'd be hard pushed to find.
He was christened on a Sunday, he was wed on a Monday,
He was buried on a Saturday afternoon,
So he went to church three times.
He always kept so busy, for God he never had the time,
So when he died on a Wednesday (a wet windy Wednesday)
He died, oh he died for all time.
Well he was so well know up and down our street,
Everybody loved our Stan,
He was a grand old chap with his afternoon nap
And his trips to the ice cream van.
Well he'd eat it with some jelly while he watched the telly,
You know he never would hurt a fly,
Making naughty suggestions to the home help
O aye...he always gave his luck a try
Well that concludes the story of our Stan
And you know it's such a blinkin' shame,
Cos it's too late to wonder, when you're six feet under,
Whether Jesus really rose again.
Well they pulled down his flat and they said 'that's that!'
Now they're building a McDonald's there
And pretty soon nobody will remember at all
The old chap who used to live there.
He was christened on a Sunday, he was wed on a Monday,
He was buried on a Saturday afternoon,

So he went to church three times.
He always kept so busy, for God he never had the time,
So when he died on a Wednesday (a wet windy Wednesday)
He died, oh he died for all time.

Chapter 8: The Hot Pot Supper

A particular (and rather peculiar) feature of northern social life is the 'Hot Pot supper'.

The existence of the hot pot, largely unknown south of a line drawn between Liverpool in the west and Hull in the east before 1960, became much more widespread with the advent of Coronation St and Betty's famous hot pot.

As far as large northern gatherings are concerned the hot pot has three unbeatable qualities: It's hot and filling (crucial on those cold northern nights), it's comparatively cheap (also crucial in a land where brass is king) and best of all...you can pay somebody else to make it and deliver it in a van. For the uninitiated a hot pot is little more than a helping of stew with a circular 'lid' of flaky pastry balanced on top of it. It's thus easy to transport still hot and steaming in great cavernous pots and ladle out at the required destination...the original fast food for the hungry northerner long before Ronald McDonald started clowning around across the pond.

As we started approaching churches to offer our services as entertainment and outreach we very quickly became familiar with the importance of this type of event.

The initial phone conversation would go something like this:

'Hello is that St Swinebury's?'

'Yes.'

'I represent a Christian band called 'Freedom'. We were wondering if we could interest you in putting on an outreach social event at which we would play free of charge.'

(Slightly puzzled silence) 'An outreach event?'(Churches aren't known for this these days)

'Yes, you know rather like a cabaret so the unchurched wouldn't be scared off.'

(Slightly alarmed tone) 'A cabaret...in church?'

'No no we were thinking more of a non church building...perhaps a function room in a pub.'

(Definite alarmed tone) 'A PUB?'

'Yes and you could lay on a hot pot supper.'

(Sudden change of tone) 'Oh well I think we should be able to manage something.'

In our experience the term 'hot pot supper' opened as many doors to churches as the key term 'free gig' did with pubs.

In our time we must have played at well over a hundred of these hotpotcentric socials. Many of them have blurred into each other through the mists of time, one of God's small mercies, but a few still stand out in the memory and none more so than the night we went to Colne.

Colne's, claim to fame now rests almost exclusively as being the home of a huge shopping outlet which started life as a converted mill selling cheap and cheerful discount goods and which has now expanded and gone upmarket so as to rival the Mall of America in its size and ability to pull in the savvy shopper in search of a bargain. When we visited in the early nineties however Colne was still in its pre-mill stage and therefore was a rather dull small Lancashire town that most people passed on the way to somewhere else.

It was a fair drive from our base in South Manchester but we had been tempted with organizer's talk of 'a hundred or so' in the audience (a very rare experience for us in those days) and so we rehearsed all our best stuff and set off on a bitter cold February night full of hope and expectation. It wasn't the easiest of drives, battling our way through heavy snow across the Pennines but when we arrived at the large church hall we were encouraged by the brightly lit interior shining out into the night, it looked warm and welcoming.

We pulled up outside the main gates and slipped and slithered our way to the entrance. As I stepped through the doorway I was greeted by the massively overweight frame of a girl who looked about fifteen. I adopted my best Christian hail fellow well met tone and asked directions to the organizer:

'Hello love can you tell me where I can find Mr Sidebottom?'

Her response was to push past me in a panic, unintentionally connecting her fist with my jaw which threw me back against the door, hitting the back of my head and felling me like a sack of potatoes.

Pandemonium broke out with people running from all directions. I remember an extremely agitated voice clearly saying:

'Who let Janet out?' but not much else.

Janet, who turned out to be thirty eight rather than fifteen, was a woman with learning difficulties and a morbid fear of men, especially unknown men. She had been brought along by her ageing parents as a special treat on the express condition, laid down by the organizing committee, that they should not leave her side at any time. I had presented myself in front of her at the exact moment when her seventy four year old mother had given up the fight with her bladder which was groaning under the strain of too many cups of tea and left her for one minute, the rest was unfortunate.

As I was sitting nursing my dislocated jaw in one of the rooms which had been set aside for the 'artistes', I was introduced to the MC for the evening, Arthur. This gent, who at a conservative estimate was pushing eighty, was dressed immaculately in white tuxedo, white frilly dress shirt and white bowtie. However he was sporting a badly fitting jet black wig which was done in the style of a seventies perm and which allowed what was left of his own white hair to stick out at the bottom on the nape of his neck. I couldn't help thinking that with a little black boot polish liberally applied to his wizened face he could have easily passed as a black and white minstrel.

Arthur, completely ignoring my suffering, launched into a detailed breakdown of the evening's planned events. The night would start with introductions and greetings (from Arthur), there would then be a quiz (conducted by Arthur) with a cash prize of £5, it would have been more Arthur explained but the vicar didn't approve of gambling, this would be followed by a game of bingo (at which the caller would be Arthur) with a star cash prize of £10 (special dispensation from the vicar), there would then be a hot pot supper followed by the turn for the evening (us) which would be introduced by, you guessed it, Arthur.

By this time the room had filled up with a group of curious helpers, who having heard about Janet's exploits, had come to see the damage for themselves...there was a lot of oohing, aahing and tutting going on.

By way of something to say I asked when we would meet the minister, meaningful glances were exchanged amongst the group, Arthur spoke up:

'He won't be joining us tonight.' I was slightly taken aback by this, all I that I could manage by way of reply was:

'Oh that's a shame.'

'Yes it is,' said Arthur. There was a protracted silence finally broken by an old lady at the back:

'We don't want him here anyhow, not after what he's done.'

She was quickly hushed and led out of the room. Before I could ask the obvious question Arthur fixed me with one of his bloodshot eyes:

'So is everything clear about the plan for the evening?'

We nodded meekly like naughty children.

'Good.' As he turned to leave I noticed for the first time how extremely bow legged he was, suddenly he stopped to offer one more item for our briefing notes:

'By the way tonight I'm using my stage name...Craig Denver.'

I frantically suppressed the urgent need to laugh by covering my mouth and pressing hard, forgetting about my jaw, the sudden agonising pain reminded me that I would need medical attention after this gig.

My encounter with Janet had seriously held us up in terms of setting up our gear, other members of the band battled heroically with the elements outside to bring everything in while I fiddled with my jaw and experimented with talking and singing in our artistes' room. Arthur was adamant that he wouldn't start the quiz until everything was ready. As my fellow band members filed back in after setting up duties I could tell something was badly wrong. It was now apparent that the 'hundred or so' referred to by the organizer on the phone referred to the average age of the audience rather than numbers, it seemed that Arthur was, by comparison, a mere whippersnapper. The other problem also referred to numbers, the blizzard raging outside had obviously made a lot of people think again about leaving their cosy firesides and Cilla Black's 'Blind Date' on TV to risk life and ageing limbs on the sheet ice, there were no more than twenty people sparsely scattered around the hall.

My heart sank.

I had been looking forward to a big gig with a hundred lively interested people, hopefully some of them non Christians whom we could reach with the Gospel. What I got was a blizzard, a visit to an old people's center, an aching jaw and nothing to look forward to except a death defying return journey through snow drifts rounded off by a visit to my local Accident & Emergency department. Quietly I raged, Job like, against God...What was the big idea? What was I being punished for? Didn't He appreciate all the work that had gone into this evening? The hours of rehearsals, done at the end of the working day when tiredness was already setting in, the time spent finding the gig in the first place, the phone calls, mail shots, follow ups, and final arrangements? Was this His idea of a joke? If it was I wasn't laughing, I'd lost my sense of humor somewhere between Janet's right upper cut and Craig Denver's briefing session.

I was in the middle of my private rant when Arthur appeared at the door; he was beaming from ear to ear.

'Look's like we've got a good turn out!'

The band looked at each other, could he be serious? Then the scales fell from my eyes, my furious remonstrations with God were further fuelled. We'd been duped, there never were going to be 'a hundred or so' in the audience, we'd merely been told that to lure us in…in reality they were delighted with twenty. I glared at Arthur, at that precise moment I could cheerfully have got hold of his white dicky bow and used it as a tourniquet to throttle him, my thoughts had taken a distinctively unChristian turn. I decided the best strategy was to get through the evening as best we could and get out of the place as soon as possible. The way the weather was going there was a danger of being snowed in if we stayed too late. This was unthinkable.

The obstacle which blocked our early departure however, apart from the millions of tons of fresh ice and snow being deposited every passing minute on the route home, was now making final adjustments to his tux and checking his wig for signs of slippage. His pace was infuriatingly leisurely, but then again why wouldn't it be? This, after all, was his big moment and he only lived round the corner. Neil the guitarist had a look of despair on his face, he muttered in my direction:

'We're here for the night!'

I knew I had to try something, the situation was urgent, I stood up and faced Arthur.

'Arthur,' I tried to sound as firm as possible but his frown reminded me that I'd made a mistake, I started again. 'Craig, I was wondering , in view of the weather and in view of my injury if you could possibly put us on earlier and do, say, the bingo and the quiz after us.'

Neil looked at me as if he could kiss me, I had brought hope back to the situation. Arthur had other ideas.

'Oh no, no,' he blustered cheerfully, 'guest turn is always top of t'bill, we wouldn't hear of anything else.'

He smiled at me as if he was doing me a big favor, once again

I sized up his dickie bow and wondered how tight it would go. I looked at the rest of the band and watched the hope leave their eyes, it was one of the saddest sights I'd ever seen. The last time I'd seen such hopelessness was years before at a Ken Dodd 'Laughter Show' when he announced to a stunned audience after nearly three hours on stage that he was only half way through. I thought I'd give it one more go.

'Not at all Craig, we don't stand on ceremony, besides it's only right that the host finishes off the evening.'

This seemed to hit the spot, Arthur paused for thought, my spirits once again started to lift, he seemed to make a decision and turned to me:

'Well, perhaps...' he got no further, at that point one of the small army of helpers hurried into the room.

'Arthur,' Arthur turned and glared at him, he started again sheepishly,"Craig, we'd better get things started, we're already running 45 minutes late and the natives are getting restless.'

I had a sudden vision of being snared and pinned to the ground by a pile of zimmer frames wielded by a gaggle of berserk senior citizens. In a flash, before I could say another word, Arthur was gone, a minute later we heard his introduction followed by the first question of his quiz:

'Now then, write down the numbers of the buses that go to Nelson from 'ere, the one with the most correct numbers wins and, just to make it a bit more tricky, you're not allowed the number eleven.'

There was a loud groan followed by a shrill female voice, the same voice that had made the mysterious comment about the minister:

'Why not?'

'Because everybody and his dog knows the number eleven goes to Nelson, that's why Edna.'

We sat in our room and listened to nineteen similarly obscure questions being laboriously read out, interspersed with various objections and tedious requests for clarifications.

Perhaps the most bizarre was:

'Name the minister in the 1950's who almost came to our church but didn't at the last minute because we wouldn't pay him what he wanted.'

All the time Dave the drummer occasionally gave nervous glances out of the window and equally nervous glances at his watch...it was now nearly nine o'clock. I noticed that our female vocalist was missing:

'Where's Joy?'

Neil shrugged; 'Dunno.'

Suddenly there was a commotion in the hall...we peeked out from behind the door to see one of the organizers in intense conversation with Arthur, who had his hand over the microphone, was it my imagination or was the color draining out of his face? He uncovered the mike:

'Ladies and gentlemen I regret to inform you that 'otpot is cancelled.'

An audible gasp went round the room:

'Apparently they're snowed in and gritters won't get down their end till at least eleven o'clock tonight.'

Everybody was shifting uncomfortably on their seats, Arthur attempted to head off the mounting panic:

'Now Jim and 'arold have kindly walked up to Wong's chippy and they can rustle up twelve meat and 'tato pies, they're fetching them in right now. I suggest we serve the ladies first, then any children and finally the gentlemen.'

Neil spoke first:

'It's Colne's answer to the feeding of the five thousand.'

'Five thousand? I wish!' I said.

Arthur was speaking again:

'Obviously twelve pies won't go round everybody but there is a full Chinese menu available.'

Once again the shrill female voice could be heard:

'Will this be included in t'price of t'ticket?'

Arthur hesitated:

'Well of course the pies will be, but you know, the Chinese is more expensive, I don't think...'

'I thought so.'

Arthur's professional composure was beginning to crack, his voice was a tone higher than before:

'Look, we'll have a game of bingo while we're waiting, and don't forget we've still got our star turn to come.'

There was a general murmuring that didn't bode well for our chances, I was beginning to get agitated.

'Where's Joy? Where's she gone all this time?' In reality whether we knew the whereabouts of our singer or not didn't make a whole lot of difference to our situation at that particular moment, it's was just that, with the whole evening threatening to crash and burn, I wanted to feel in control of *something*.

Finally, post quiz, post pies, post bingo, post interval, at long last our turn came, Joy reappeared with two minutes to spare and we went on stage at a quarter to ten. We had already had a council of war about our running order and, as the evening wore on, the play list had got shorter and shorter. By the time we hit the stage we were planning to play just five songs, we never made it. Half way through the third song, as if in response to a hidden signal half the audience got up and exited out the back, Arthur stepped briskly up to the mike at the end of the song to wind things up, it was the shortest gig we ever did.

Back in the 'artistes' room we just looked at each other in stunned amazement, what had prompted such a mass walk out? Were we really that bad? The arrival of Arthur solved the mystery:

'Thanks very much, sorry about the sudden ending but the Ring n' Ride bus wasn't prepared to wait past ten o'clock.'

So that was it, we'd battled through snowstorms, suffered personal injury, waited around for hours to play, only to be cut off in our prime by the free bus service for the elderly that had been booked for ten o'clock and was driven by a jobsworth who wouldn't wait another moment. Our evening was complete.

I couldn't have felt worse as we loaded the gear back in the van for the homeward trek, my jaw was killing me, Arthur came to see us off at the door.

'Thanks a lot, we enjoyed it very much and hope you'll come again.' Then a little more sheepishly, 'I'm sorry that things didn't go quite to plan.' His tone became conspiratorial as he produced a large white paper bag and stuffed it into my hands:

'I had a few more pies than I told that lot,' he nodded in the direction of the hall, 'I thought you might like them for the journey home. I'm sorry they're a bit squashed but 'arold slipped on the ice on his way from the chippy.'

I forced my aching jaw into something resembling a smile as I took the bag from him, I could feel the contents forming one congealed stone cold lump in my hands.

'Thanks Arthur, they'll come in handy on the trip.' ('for ballast' I thought privately.)

We slalomed precariously through the narrow streets until we finally reached the bright lights of the motorway that would take us home. As I was trying to find somewhere to stuff the bag of congealed pies I suddenly remembered something:

'So come on Joy where did you get to for over an hour?'

Joy told us that, bored with our collective moaning, she had decided to go and sit out front with the audience. She had ended up sitting next to an old lady who was on her own at a small table and they'd struck up a conversation. Doreen lived on her own and had done since her husband had died some twenty years before, her three grown up daughters had all done well for themselves married and flown the nest. Although they lived in the area she very rarely saw them or her grandchildren. She often wondered if she had done something wrong when they were children that meant they didn't want to be near her now. She was lonely and had come along because the minister had popped round and had invited her, it was the first time she'd met him…besides she didn't like Cilla Black, her voice grated on her.

As the various catastrophes of cancelled hotpots and overlong quizzes came and went Joy and Doreen became engrossed in conversation. Doreen was well aware of the Bible stories, she had gone to Sunday School as a child but had lost touch when she had left school at fourteen and had to get a job in one of the mills. She was married at sixteen and had her three children in close succession, there was no time for church. Joy took the opportunity of refreshing Doreen's memory about some of the great Gospel messages that she needed to hear again, about how God cares for each one of us and values us personally, and about how, since we all have the one Father, we are all brothers and sisters in Christ and therefore a family…a family that Doreen belonged to.

They had exchanged addresses and Joy had promised to keep in touch, she had also drawn the attention of one of the church elders to Doreen who had introduced himself to her. Joy finished up with a remark that set me thinking:

'If you lot hadn't wanted to play at the end I could have talked to Doreen some more.'

I thought back to my self righteous rant at God when things started going wrong, I realized that my reactions had been all about *me*, what *I* wanted to get out of the evening, what *I* considered would make the trip and preparations worth while, the needs of the folk who had turned out that night had come way down my list. I also realized, to my amazement, that if the evening *had* gone to plan it would have meant all of us staying backstage and Joy would probably have never met Doreen, and even if she had, would certainly not have had the time she had with her.

As we continued our slow journey homeward I realized that God had been asking something of us that night. 'I know that bands enjoy themselves more when they have a big crowd, but will you do this special job for me? There's this one lady who hasn't been anywhere near other Christians or church for a long time, but tonight she's come to have a look see. She needs to talk to somebody younger, somebody who could be one of the daughters she misses so much. Would you put up with delays and frustrations tonight so that I can get one of you alongside her? I want to talk with her one to one.'

I felt humbled and slightly ashamed but so pleased that I had seen for myself how God really can take *any* situation and use it how He pleases.

It was a demonstration that God would make over and over again in the course of our time on the road.

There is a brief, but fascinating postscript to this story. After holding out for about a week after the gig I succumbed to plain nosiness and phoned Arthur. I needed to know the reason for some of the folk that night reacting so badly to my question about the minister's absence. What had he done? I imagined all sorts of evils and perversions. The reality was that he had forgotten to put the names of two of the parishioners on the distribution list for Harvest food parcels, so they had gone without for a couple of days until his mistake had come to light. The fact that he had immediately rushed round to their houses with food bought out of his own pocket had not atoned for his sin in the eyes of some.

The astonishing thing was that one of these omitted people was Doreen, the lady Joy had spoken to, who quite clearly bore no grudge at all. On the contrary, she hadn't even mentioned the food parcel issue to Joy at all. If the minister *had* remembered to put her name on the list, she would have received no visit from him and no personal invitation. Almost certainly she wouldn't have come and Joy wouldn't have got to meet her. Once again God had arranged everything and, in spite of the weather, in spite of our own impatience, in spite of Arthur's inflexibility, in spite of being hotpotless...He had come alongside Doris just as He intended, just as He'd planned.

THE CHURCHGOER'S CHA CHA

There's not a day goes by
That I don't pray for those inferior to me
The non churchgoers who've never sung
A rousing chorus of 'Majesty'.
Church I'm never away
Sunday service night and day
And during open prayer
I'm always the first and last to pray.
Monday Bible study, which of course I lead
Tuesday Alpha group, which, of course, I don't need
Wednesday house group, at my house naturally,
Thursday church meeting
When I'm in charge of everything, including tea.
Friday I'm in the choir
Saturday a meeting just for men
And then before you know it
It's Sunday
And the whole lot starts again!
As for good works, well modesty forbids
But let's just say I run the youth group
And I knock myself out for those kids.
When my turn comes
They'll open up those pearly gates
cos the Lord will be greeting
One of his closest and dearest mates.
Now I get angry
With some people I meet
Forever talking about Jesus
And how they're not worthy to kiss His feet.
They just don't understand
The gospel as well as me
But that's not surprising, not everyone gets to be...
A Pharisee!

Chapter 9: Crossfire

Since I had been saved at 'Greenbelt' in 1983, it's not surprising then that this kind of Christian meeting had a special place in my heart. I loved the atmosphere, the fellowship, the chance to relax and enjoy yourself in the company of like minded people. So when we were invited to play at Merseyside's version of Greenbelt, 'Crossfire', in 1991 I was genuinely thrilled.

By this time 'Freedom' had been going for about five years and was already in its third incarnation , a three piece comprising a female vocalist: Joy; myself on keyboards and vocals and Alan on guitar. At this stage in the game I was still personally very ambitious…playing it cool but secretly longing for some kind of recognition.

However it's fair to say that when we packed up our stuff and set off in convoy for Aintree, it was more in hope than expectation.

We certainly weren't the headline act, in fact in terms of headlines we were struggling to even get a line or two in miniscule font somewhere buried on page 23 of the festival programme. Nevertheless my sense of self importance as we chugged our way down the M62 was indomitable. I cheered myself with the thought that even Cliff had had to start somewhere. In spite of our lack of international acclaim so far I was convinced it was only a matter of time. I was writing good songs, I reasoned, and my fellow band members were talented, though not quite as much as me naturally, maybe this would be our big break. This thought even overcame my disappointment in the weather which was now decidedly damp.

This self satisfaction continued as we arrived, being allowed , as artistes you understand, to drive straight onto the showground and not have to queue up with the riff raff at the main entrance. The smugness took its first knock however as we were ushered to our allotted parking space, a muddy patch of ground about a mile from where we were to play and right next to the toilet cubicles. As I got out of the car I saw that it had already settled under the weight of our gear a good three or four inches into a small lake of water, or at least I hoped it was water.

We decided to do a reccy of the site, wandering around we found the usual assortment of marquees and stages, stalls and arenas. The market stall area was largely populated by gentlemen with large bushy beards selling handcrafted leatherwork and women in long Kaftans purveying various dodgy products from the fringes of spiritual life. Leaflets rejoicing in titles such as 'Raike and home groups...the way forward?' and artefacts such as pipe holders decorated with an assortment of Celtic crosses competed for space with wooden wall plaques with messages such as 'Open every door, look out of every window'. I resolved to buy one of those for our nosy neighbours back home.

We searched eagerly for the stage we had been told we would play on but after half an hour of aimless wandering still had not found it. Finally I buttonholed a passing steward who didn't know where it was either and had to consult mission HQ on her walkie talkie.

Ah yes, we were told, there had been a slight glitch and the stage hadn't turned up yet, therefore we had been reassigned to a tent originally intended to be a café. The guy on the radio was very apologetic.

I was secretly quite pleased about this as the weather was deteriorating and I quite fancied the idea of an indoor venue, I didn't really understand why the organizers should be so apologetic about it. When we finally found the tent in question I understood. A marquee it was not, it was much more like a large family sized camping tent with one side lifted up. We would be playing in this 'doorway' to an audience outside on the grass. Moreover, since no one had originally intended this to be a music venue when the plans were draw up, the tent was located right next to one of the large stages with its 5000 watt output speakers. The only way our audience would know what we were singing would be if we had someone to sign for us…I was livid.

We immediately held an extraordinary general meeting…my two fellow band members were better Christians than I and tried to put a positive spin on it.

'At least lots of people will see us 'cos we're near the main stage even if they can't hear us,' offered Joy.

'Yeah that's right,' Alan added, 'and we can hand out leaflets!'

I was in a cynical mood:

'Oh good, then we can print the lyrics in case they can't lip read.'

I wasn't going to give up so easy and headed for the main administration tent to make my case. I wasn't filled with confidence when I arrived, the tent was filled with people milling around four or five desks manned by harassed looking staff hunched over lists and site plans, it was clear I wasn't the only one with a problem. I joined one of the long queues at the desks, in front of me was an older couple in their mid fifties, they were both dressed more for a day at the office than a camping weekend, alongside the rest of the scruffy youth milling about they stood out like two sore thumbs. I was curious about them and attempted to strike up a conversation.

'So…here just for the day or are you camping?'

The woman looked at me in alarm:

'No, we aren't camping. In fact that's why we're here, we want to ask about alternative accommodation.'

I was puzzled:

'Alternative accommodation?'

'Yes, you know like chalets or something.'

Now I was really puzzled:

'I'm afraid there aren't any chalets here, just a camping ground. Haven't you brought a tent?'

'No we haven't, we didn't need one last year.'

I was beginning to twig:

'Where were you last year?'

'Spring Harvest, in Minehead.'

'Ah yes,' I said knowingly, 'that's because it's held at Butlins isn't it? As you can see," I gestured to the view of muddy fields from the doorflap 'no Butlin's here.'

Up to this point the woman had done all the talking, my revelation seemed to jog the man out of his reverie, he looked directly at me for the first time, as if this was all my fault:

'We're only here to see Cliff Richard.' He continued to stare at me, somewhat manically I thought. I broke the bad news.

'Cliff Richard isn't coming to Crossfire.'

The couple exchanged horrified looks, once again I was addressed in an accusatory tone:

'Are you sure?'

'Absolutely positive.'

There was a long silence as the couple pondered my statement. I decided at this point to give up my own quest as the queue hadn't moved an inch in twenty minutes. As I turned to go , they began to follow me, I accelerated slightly, to my relief they slowed to a halt. As I hurried back to the others I could hear the man asking a hapless passer by whether Cliff Richard was appearing that weekend, he was obviously in denial.

I was astonished at this couple's complete and utter lack of awareness. The only other time I had come across such completely misdirected expectation was fifteen years previously when I had been living in Egypt. I was taking a friend to see the pyramids and while actually *inside* the famous long gallery of Khufu's pyramid I had been accosted by an American tourist with the enquiry 'Hey, which way to the john?'

When I rejoined the others we agreed that there was nothing to be done except get on with it and hope for the best...maybe there might be a power cut...maybe the act on the main stage would take pity on us and shut up for just long enough for the audience to hear one of our songs…maybe Cliff might show up after all and ask us to back him on stage.

I wasn't too happy for the rest of the morning, the smiles of my hairy brothers in Christ behind the stalls left me cold and, to be brutally honest, when I overheard one of the worship leaders exhorting his flock 'to share with the person next to you how you feel', I came close to snatching the burger from the hands of a passing youth that he'd just paid £5 for and pushing it up his nose.

Not for the first time I engaged God in urgent conversation:

Why, I wanted to know, was He screwing up our big chance? Didn't He realize that a good performance here could be the break I had been waiting for over five years? How were we ever going to be known now?

In my state of abject self pity I was convinced that things couldn't get worse, I was wrong.

When the allotted hour came for us to perform we found, to our horror, that one of the headline acts, 'Eden Burning', was already in mid set with a large audience of adoring fans. As we struck up our first chord some of them turned to look at us with the same expression on their faces I imagined people might have when staring at someone who had noisily broken wind during a funeral service. Things went downhill from there, my witty banter fell on deaf ears, well no ears at all actually, and Alan's best guitar licks wafted on the ether, unheard and unappreciated . It was, as far as I was concerned, a disaster.

As we packed up I found myself having a further extremely intense conversation with God;

Why had he wasted our time like this? What, I further enquired, was the point in causing us this much humiliation and when, I demanded, would we see some glimmer of success? I wasn't listening for an answer, too busy in my mental rantings, but as I shoved the last bag of leads into the boot of the car a thought occurred to me. When we had first arrived I had noticed, with some pity, a long line of people queuing for water at a stand pipe that had been set up. At the time I had thought no more of it, busily searching as I was for our prime parking spot. Now that mental picture flashed back into my mind, a long line of people going nowhere for at least ten minutes or so while they waited their turn...a ready made audience.

I turned to my crestfallen comrades, I was excited:

'I've got an idea !' I said.

Within an hour we had found the stand pipe, with an even longer queue than before, set up our gear facing the line, borrowed a portable generator from a bemused technician and were busy blasting out a selection of our greatest hits.

I'll never know whether it was out of sympathy, rather as you put a small coin into the collecting tin of a busker at a cinema queue or whether out of genuine interest, but as we played and after we finished, a steady stream of people came up enquiring about us. By the end of the afternoon we had firm bookings for four concerts all over the region and enquiries for lots more.

One minister told me much later that he had booked us because he liked our 'entrepreneurial spirit' which I think is church speak for 'sheer nerve'.

My own theory however is less flattering, I came to realize, that my spirit of self satisfaction and self importance had needed to be broken before anything useful could be done with me or through me. It was only when this process was complete and I was approaching something like humility that I was fit for purpose.

As usual God knew exactly what he was doing that wet day at Crossfire and I'm sure that we made more contacts that day and eventually played to a lot more people than we would ever have done otherwise.

That day also marked a turning point in the history of the band. I wasn't the only one to realize what God had been up to and the other band members also realized that our real purpose from then on was to put aside personal ambition and play purely and simply to the glory of God. Not that we always succeeded, as this book testifies, but at least we knew what now what we were *supposed* to be doing.

That festival is long gone now, having run out of steam and money sometime in the mid nineties but I never forgot the lesson I learnt there. I tried to share it on several occasions with other similarly self satisfied Christian performers who were waiting for the inevitability of international stardom…with varying amounts of success, some listened, some didn't, but for those who didn't I couldn't help thinking that God had a patch of muddy grass waiting for them sometime soon.

Chapter 10: The Working Men's Club

A grim night in a small Northern town. The rain swept horizontally down the steep street of terraced houses as we struggled with the heavy equipment, unloading from cars and dumping speakers and bags of gear unceremoniously inside the porch of the club.

This was a working men's club...a phenomenon unknown in the south but an institution in the north of the UK. It had been surprisingly simple to get this particular gig, one phone call to the concert secretary (*a quaint old name for the guy who did the bookings*) with repeated use of the phrase 'free of charge' had done the trick (for further details on this technique see appendix 1). I had a sneaking feeling that once heard, this phrase had blocked all other content...so that other phrases such as 'Christian band' 'Gospel songs' and 'Ministry' had passed him by like the twitter of bird song.

When we got inside it was near impossible to see the stage from the rear entrance through the blue funk of fag smoke that hung in the air like nuclear fallout. The room was long and narrow, just like a nuclear bunker in fact, small wooden round tables were dotted about, each with a selection of gnarled punters who eyed us suspiciously as we made our way through and started setting up. I tried to ease things by smiling pointedly at one or two people, but this only seemed to deepen their suspicion. I heard snatches of muttered comments 'bloody Christians' and 'What's Colin playing at?' (Colin being the Concert Secretary I had sucked up to on the phone).

It took about half an hour to set up and then we needed a brief sound check. Unfortunately this clashed with the timing of the cash bingo and my polite requests to ask if the start could be delayed by five minutes to allow us to do the check were met with a brisk retort:

'Delay t'bingo. Don't talk daft lad. It's twenty quid prize tonight!' Colin was obviously not a man to be trifled with and we bided our time, going over the running order, whispering in a corner as bingo cards were sold and the bingo machine was rolled out onto the stage.

This machine was basically a glass box on legs full of balls with a funnel at the top. On being plugged in the balls started bouncing around the box finding their way out through the funnel at the top, one by one. It was obvious that this contraption had seen heavy service since about 1958. We waited for the game to begin, but it soon became evident by the way first one, then two and finally three club officials were peering into the box and carrying on an animated discussion that something was up. Finally one of them walked up to the mike at the front of the stage and tapped it loudly:

'Testing, Testing...can you hear me?'

'Yes we bloody can Albert, get on with it,' came a voice from the back.

'I'm sorry to say that, like happened last Christmas, some joker has nicked the balls again.'

At this news, two old dears who had been sitting more or less comatose up to this point suddenly sparked into life, one of them stood up waving her bingo card in the air:

'What about my £1.50? I paid £1.50 for this card!'

Albert rounded on her like a rear gunner on a WW II Lancaster bomber:

'Be quiet Doris...we've got a crisis here and you going on don't help.'

I turned to Neil the guitarist...

'It's going to be a long night,' I said wearily.

Eventually the balls were surrendered by a grinning pensioner.

(Comment from Doris as the frail old man handed over the missing items:

'You know your trouble Frank...you've never grown up.') and the game proceeded, followed by the obligatory shout of: 'Meat pies are now available from the bar.'

At last we were on, the lights in the hall were lowered and a couple of spots shone down on us as Colin took the stage to introduce us:

'And now Ladies and Gentlemen we have our turn for the evening, something a bit different tonight...'

He paused for dramatic effect, from out of the darkness I heard a loud:

'Ey up!' a particularly northern exclamation with the kind of intonation reserved for the kind of occasion when your companion had just stepped in a pile of dog mess.

Pretending he hadn't heard what everybody else clearly had, Colin continued unperturbed:

'Yes folks tonight we have a Gospel group...so put your hands together and give a warm welcome to...'

There was a momentary pause, in that split second Colin realized that he had forgotten the name of the band, but this minor detail wasn't going to spoil things...with a piece of brilliant mental agility which I later pieced together for myself he recalled what he *did* know about us...a Christian group and my name...Scott Fellows...he continued triumphantly, 'The Scott Fellowship!'

We looked at each other in stunned silence for a moment before I wrenched myself back to the opening chord I was supposed to be playing and the performance began.

As we worked our way through our set we sensed the distinct chill we had first picked up from the audience starting to thaw a little and by the time we took our customary twenty minute break at the half way point things were on a much friendlier basis. People had begun to clap and sing along and to laugh in all the right places.

As I stood at the bar trying to get a drink Colin appeared at my side:

'Let me get that,' he beamed, nodding to the barman. He continued in a hail fellow well met tone:

'To be honest Scott I thought you were going to be crap, but actually you're not bad. Have you been doing this long?'

I hesitated over my answer as I was still trying to figure out whether I had just been insulted or not.

'Well yes, about seven years actually.'

'Bloody amazing!'

Again I had no idea what Colin meant by that response but I had the feeling it wasn't positive. With a hearty slap to the back he moved off to insult another unsuspecting punter, leaving me deep in thought.

As things were going well we decided to get the second half going with one of our most popular songs 'Just One More'. This was a combination of two predominant themes in my life; a deep love of Jesus coupled with my personal dislike of Country and Western music which made for a pretty heady theological cocktail. It had that slow depressing C&W swing beat combined with the mournful sound of slide guitars that slowly drains the will to live out of you as the song progresses. I gave it its usual introduction, offering counselling for any country and western fans out there and, for those hardliners who had progressed on to line dancing, the phone number of a good rehab clinic. This didn't get the laughs it normally got but I pressed on regardless:

JUST ONE MORE
(sung with Southern States drawl, repeat phrases in brackets)
My idea of hell is singing country
Round that big bonfire that burns below (burns below)
After each song ends you know the Devil (the Devil)
Would shout out…
Yep…I think there's time for just one more.
You know Jesus was a man like you and me

He found out just how cruel life could be
He died so he could set men free
To go to heaven for eternity
And not have to go to Nashville Tennessee
You know friends Country is a recent invention
No cowboys roamed the plains of Galilee
So when I go to praise the Lord
In heaven I never will be bored
Cos heaven will be Dolly and Tammy free.
What will you say to Him on that last day
When he asks 'Why did you never believe in me boy?'
Cos if you can't come up with somethin' good,
If you didn't live life like you should,
You'll be singing 'Tie a yellow ribbon' for eternity!

Now normally, during this song, we would encourage the audience to sing along with the repeats at the end of each line of the chorus which always produced a lot of hilarity...not on this occasion however.

No matter how much I cajoled, teased or joked we were met with a stone wall of silence. This was in such marked contrast to the reaction to other songs we had done in the first half that it really put us off our stride. I think it's fair to say that the second half was a lot shorter than the first after that song and we only received a smattering of polite applause to our big finish number 'Oh Happy Day'.

As we came off stage in a state of bemusement the ubiquitous Colin was waiting for me, this time he wasn't smiling, gripping my arm firmly he yanked me to one side and hissed into my ear:

'You'll not play here again lad!'

I tried to play it cool:

'Is there a problem Colin?'

'Problem? PROBLEM?' The hiss had become a shout, 'Look at that wall!'

I followed his accusing finger which was pointing at a large silver plaque on the rear wall, it took a moment in the dim light to get my eyes to focus on the writing, finally I could make out the lovingly engraved inscription:

North West Headquarters
Country and Western Appreciation Society

I looked at Colin, he looked as if he was about to have a heart attack, I could see the headline now:

'Concert Secretary killed by shock, Christian band leader on manslaughter charge...'

I felt as if I should say something, all I managed was a feeble sounding:

'Sorry.'

'Sorry! It's too late for that lad! Far too late! You've insulted every member of this club!

What in the bloody hell were you thinking of?'

In that moment I realized that in fact I hadn't been thinking at all. So self satisfied was I with my own wit in lyric writing that it had never crossed my mind that people might actually be hurt or insulted by them. Just because I hated Country and Western with a passion didn't mean that everybody else did, sooner or later I had been bound to meet an audience who wouldn't appreciate the joke...that day had now arrived.

We decided to make a sharp exit, covering our tactical retreat with profuse apologies. I have a vivid memory of Colin's scowl filling my rear view mirror through the rain as we drove off into the night.

On the way home I started to feel upset, I had done the Lord a disservice and left people with a negative memory of what was supposed to be hopeful, joyous Christian witness set to music. I had neglected to follow Jesus' example of communicating with people on a level they would understand and with subject matter that was familiar and important to them. As far as I recall, for example, he never went out of his way to belittle shepherds.

The lyrics of this song had been written as a joke, but I had not been careful enough in checking out who I was singing to and the joke had rebounded on me.

From that night on I resolved to be much aware of the kind of people we were playing to and select our songs appropriately...I also developed a compulsive habit of scanning the walls in a new venue before I played a note.

Chapter 11: The Shopping Mall

What could be a better opportunity to spread the word than to play in a shopping mall?

This was the question in my mind as I eagerly accepted the invitation from a local vicar to play in a shopping center just outside Manchester a couple of Saturdays before Christmas. He was quite open about the purpose of the event:

'I want to get the buggers back into church on Sundays instead of raping, looting and pillaging their way round Tesco and Argos.'

Quite to the point I thought, I could do business with this man.

And so the arrangements were made, his congregation were keen, I was told, and would turn out to help and sing along with carols. Now it must be said at this point that, second to Country and Western of course, Christmas carols are my most disliked sacred musical form. They are responsible for painting such a misleading and inaccurate picture of Jesus' birth that to this day many people still have the belief that Jesus was born in a squeaky clean manger, surrounded by cutesy animals and adoring hordes sporting freshly laundered kaftans.

Not only that but, as we are told in one of the most loved carols, it was, according to Christina Rossetti, snowing at the time:

In the bleak midwinter, frosty wind made moan,
Earth stood hard as iron, water like a stone
Snow had fallen snow on snow, snow on snow,
In the bleak midwinter, long ago.

Now if Jesus had been born in Colne I could go along with this from bitter personal experience, but the Middle East? The

Victorians have a lot to answer for.

I shared my misgivings with Derek the Vicar, his reply was, once again, pithy:

'Don't worry about it, play what you like, most of them aren't listening to the music anyway…it's just a way of getting their attention while we nobble them.'

It's this kind of Christian encouragement that keeps struggling evangelists going in those dark moments when they ask themselves whether it's all worth it. I resolved to take Derek at his word and planned a set of music which was mainly our own material with one or two carols thrown in to keep the traditionalists happy.

Needless to say, on the Saturday in question, it was raining. I was quite unperturbed however as I had checked out this scenario with Derek and had been assured that, although there were parades of shops outside, the part we would be in was under cover, under a glass roof in fact. This was crucial, our gear was high voltage and didn't mix well with water, and though I looked forward to meeting Jesus at the end of my days, I didn't really want to meet him with my hair standing on end, a shocked expression on my face and smoke wafting out of every orifice..

The first hint of trouble came as we arrived on site, the nearest parking place was a good 400 metres from where we were playing and, except for the last 50 metres, the route was exposed to the rain which was now cranking itself up from light shower to cats and dogs status. I could just make out in the distance the figure of a sodden Derek walking toward us, he was on his own. I rolled down the window:

'Hi, where's the help?'

'They're coming along later because of the weather, but don't worry I can do some shifting.'

Derek obviously didn't grasp the problem, I enlightened him:

'If this gear gets wet it's going to be too dangerous, isn't there some way of getting nearer?'

'I don't think so.' I wasn't giving up that easy:

'There must be, how do they make deliveries? There'll be a service road somewhere. Can you ask somebody?'

I was aware that I was sitting in my nice dry car holding a conversation with somebody who had that 'fresh out of the canal' look, and now I was asking him to walk another kilometre in the rain. This thought obviously had occurred to Derek as well, but to my eternal shame I was listening to the little goblin sitting on my shoulder and he was saying:

'Look, you're doing *him* a favour here, this is *his* event, why should you get soaked just because he can't organize proper access? Let him go and sort it out and stay where you are.'

I looked at my bandmates, they were noticeably quieter than usual and avoiding eye contact...I figured they could hear my goblin as well, I rolled the window up and turned on the heater.

Derek disappeared back into the rain and was gone for what seemed like an age, when he finally reappeared he had another man with him. I rolled the window down again, Derek introduced his companion:

'This is Mr Jacobson the center manager, he's kindly agreed to let you park in one of the service bays which is under cover and only about 100 metres from where you're playing.'

We followed our new friend's directions and found ourselves in a large cavernous loading bay at the back of a supermarket. We started unloading our gear: speakers, amplifiers, guitars, keyboards, watched by a slightly bemused group of supermarket staff, some of whom were busy unloading huge packs of nappies from the back of a lorry while the others stood around chatting and smoking under a huge sign that said 'NO SMOKING.' One of them shouted across to us:

'Are you playing in the store?'

I shouted back:

'No outside in the mall.'

I was miffed to see my questioner turn to one of the others and give the thumbs up.

'The youth of today!' I thought to myself.

By the time everything was set up we were already running nearly an hour late. A trickle of people had shown up from Derek's church, mostly within the last ten minutes and long after all the heavy shifting had been done. It was probably just as well as the majority were pensioners, with one or two looking decidedly frail, I decided it would be as much as they could manage to lift a carol sheet for an hour. There was one exception to this birthday enriched group, a young man of about twenty years of age who turned up late, full of excuses that his shift at work had been extended at the last minute. James had a really positive attitude and was ready to help in any way he could in between repeatedly apologising for being late and 'letting people down'. I took an instant liking to James, as I did to anyone in fact who offered to help with the gear. He seemed genuinely enthusiastic and full of spirit.

At this point Derek introduced me to Katherine, a rather prim looking middle aged woman who was obviously an important person in the church. As Katherine stood beside Derek, sizing me and the rest of the band up, he filled me in:

'Katherine is one of the senior members of the church council, she will be doing all the introductions between songs, have you got a running order you can let her have?'

This wasn't part of our agreement, Derek saw the look on my face and added hurriedly:

'She's very good at this kind of thing.'

I looked at Derek, his demeanor reminded me of those poor souls you see on the news who have been seized by various fanatical organizations and forced, at gunpoint, to read out statements praising their kidnappers' cause. I wasn't happy, I was used to chatting with the audience between songs, maybe getting a few laughs and breaking the ice so people would listen to the really important stuff...the Gospel. All of that was now under

threat, I decided to be charming, I gave Katherine a big smile:
Now Kath...'

'Katherine,' came the swift correction. I kept smiling:

'Katherine, of course...now Katherine thank you very much
for your offer of help but..." I got no further:

'Don't mention it, now if you can let me look at the list of
carols...I like to be prepared and Derek didn't have a list to give
me.' She threw a look at Derek, who in turn looked at me, with a
look that said: 'Kill me now.'

'I'd love to be a fly on the wall at his church council meetings,'
I thought to myself. What had happened to the forthright,
assertive Derek that I'd had several conversations with on the
phone? I would have to leave that question unanswered for the
moment as there were more pressing matters to hand, I tried one
more time to save my witty banter:

'Well I don't have a list as such, I tend to leave things flexible
and see where the Spirit leads.'

Katherine gave me a long look before uttering her one word
response:

'Extraordinary.'

I got the feeling she didn't mean it in a good way. Derek dived
in:

'Katherine why don't you help the rest of the folks with the
carol sheets and the tracts, they're going to need someone like
you to organize them.'

This was a master stroke, Katherine trotted off to the group of
people who had been milling aimlessly around while we
negotiated, within moments I saw her manoeuvring them into
position, she was happy.

Derek turned to me;

'Shall we get started Scott?' he was obviously keen to get
underway before Katherine could return, I was only too happy to
oblige but first had one more piece of technical stuff to take care
off. I reached into my kit bag and lovingly took out our newest

purchase, a radio microphone. I gave it to Derek: 'If you ask one of the group to hold that it will pick up their voices and really boost the sound.'

'Great,' said Derek and immediately went over and passed it to Katherine. This wasn't quite what I'd had in mind but it was too late, Katherine had obviously decided that she had been given this to facilitate her organizer role and for a few seconds, before I could reach the volume control, the mall was treated to her orders for troop deployment:

'Albert move forward, I need short people in the middle; Nellie if you're going to stand *there* then you'll have to stop eating *that* won't you?' and so on.

One of the group, obviously overcome with the possibility of real power for one of the first times in her life grabbed the radio mike and shouted out:

'The future's bright, the future's Orange!'

This produced a temporary stunned silence and very strange looks from passers by, who of course were now having their long time suspicions that Christians were a bunch of nutters confirmed in the most dramatic way. Katherine surgically removed the mike from Mrs Orange's grasp and pushed her to the back, it was the only time that afternoon that I was pleased she was there.

At long last, we made a start, playing a selection of our own songs, which admittedly weren't particularly Christmassy. Since we hadn't played any carols yet, Katherine's commandos were a little redundant, standing in perfectly symmetrical formation behind us and gazing hopefully at their carol sheets as if the lyrics to the rock anthems we were playing might magically appear before them. Eventually it was time for something that at least mentioned Christmas, we played 'Christmas Time':

CHRISTMAS TIME

(slow and solemn in style of church choir anthem)
Christmas time is here again get the decorations in
There's special offers everywhere
Buy one get one free
Only ten more shopping days
The time just passes in a daze
Thank God for the Christmas club
It makes things easier.
Santa's in his grotto now
With a smile for you and me
Got to get the kids the latest DVD
Get a card for Aunty May
(because she sent one yesterday)
Thank God Christmas comes
But once a year.
Christmas time is here again
It's time to get the turkey in
Carol singers everywhere, getting in the way,
I'd like to give them all a tip
To keep religion out of it
And let the rest get on with it
TO GET THE SHOPPING IN.
AMEN

Quite a few of the shoppers missed a stride as they passed and heard something they weren't normally used to hearing from carol singers. I was pleased, this was the affect I wanted. To make people stop for just one second and think about what they were doing as they scurried around on the commercial Christmas treadmill. I glanced behind me to Katherine's combat troops, they were looking even more bemused than the shoppers. It was time to put them out of their misery and sing a traditional carol before they all drifted home to watch 'Countdown' on TV.

'OK everyone, we're going to sing a carol I'm sure you all know now. While Shepherds Watched...and I want you all to sing along just as if you were back at Stalag 17...I mean Pontins holiday camp.'

My little joke, feeble as it was, raised a smile with one or two passers by, I was just beginning to get somewhere to start to build some kind of rapport with the audience out there. It never got a chance to develop, as I played the introduction I became aware of some other singing coming from just outside the covered section of the mall and getting louder. I stopped playing to listen, it was the unmistakeable sound of an acoustic guitar and voices singing a carol. I was puzzled and looked over to Derek, he too was looking in the direction of the music, his expression was one of anger. Just then, still singing, a group of about fifteen people came through the automatic doors into the space we were in with someone strumming loudly on guitar bringing up the rear, they were in the middle of a rendition of 'O come all ye faithful!'

Derek had moved to the side of my keyboard, I heard him say to no one in particular;

'I don't believe it, it's the Penties!'

I folded my arms and awaited instructions, clearly we couldn't both be playing in the same space at the same time. Derek moved forward to talk to the man who was obviously the leader of the other group, the body language didn't look too hopeful, especially as I could see both men's faces going redder and redder. Eventually Derek stalked back to our group, he didn't look too happy:

'It's the Penties, they say they booked this before us, I'm not prepared to get into an argument in the middle of the shopping mall so I'm terribly sorry but we'll have to pack up.'

I was aghast:

'Just a minute! Just a minute! Surely we can work something out, can't we take turns or if they've got a music book we can play their stuff and we can all sing together.'

Derek looked at me as if I had just suggested a sing-song with Beelzebub and all his hosts, he was back in assertive mode:

'I don't think so.'

There was no further discussion, we packed up to the musical accompaniment of the Pentecostal church from down the road, having played precisely four songs and no carols. James was a star, running backward and forward carrying the vast bulk of our gear single handed with no word of complaint. We were very grateful to him as we were heavy hearted and lacking in energy.

Katherine, of course, was disgusted with the whole thing and confided in me as she returned our radio mike that this wasn't the first time that 'that church' had been so unhelpful. The last sight I had of her she was shooing her flock out of the mall, in the opposite direction to the 'Penties'.

Derek was also anxious to go, perhaps because he was angry, perhaps because he was embarrassed at being involved in such a monumental pig's ear. As soon as he saw that the gear was loaded he took his leave with an apology and a promise to rebook us 'sometime next year'. It never happened.

As I was collecting my music and doing a final check around for anything we had left behind, I was approached by the leader of the other church. They had taken a break by now and he obviously wanted to take the opportunity of having a quick word:

'Sorry about that,' he said, 'but it's not the first time that we've had a problem with Derek, it's been going on for ages.'

I couldn't help myself, I had to say something:

'Wouldn't it be better then if you consulted one another about your plans? Worked together on common projects instead of separately, I believe you're just down the road from each other aren't you?'

He spoke slowly, thoughtfully, as if a glimmer of light was beginning to penetrate the darkness:

'Well...yes...that might be possible...' and then the glimmer died out, 'but no, it really isn't that simple, if you lived here you'd realize that. Ah well nice to meet you, perhaps you could come and play for us sometime.'

That never happened either.

That left me and James on our own, with the other band members waiting in the van. I thanked him profusely, I asked him how he came to be going to that church, where he was so heavily outnumbered by much older people, his answer stunned me:

'Because if people like me abandon churches like that then they're finished aren't they? I used to go to the Pentecostal, but they've got plenty of young people there, they don't need me.'

I was curious to know a little more about him, he was a student at University but on Saturdays he worked in the mall to make some extra cash.

'Oh yes, where do you work?' I asked casually.

He pointed towards the supermarket, the one we were parked at the back of, the one whose young staff I had been so dismissive of:

'Over there.'

Now it was my turn to be embarrassed, although James would never know why.

We turned to walk back to the van and as we did so a middle aged woman came up to me:

'You've just been singing and playing the keyboards haven't you?'

'Yes,' I said.

'You're a Christian aren't you?'

'Yes,' I said, could this be a chance to witness I wondered? Her tone became sharp:

'What you said about Pontins was bang out of order, me and my kids have had a lot of good holidays there, you should know better, being a vicar.'

She was gone before I could say a word.

I'd had enough, I just wanted to get in the van and go home. There hadn't been a lot of Christmas cheer that day and, ironically, it was the Christians that had spoilt the party. Sadly this was just one of many such examples of internecine feuding between denominations we came across over the years and it was always the non Christians who missed out.

It was the non Christians who wouldn't get to come to a social because local churches couldn't agree on the details ; non Christians who would miss out on sending their kids to a church youth group because the local churches were squabbling about who would pay for the youth worker; non Christians who would remain unsaved because different denominations couldn't put their theological differences temporarily aside to enable them to cooperate on organizing a large Gospel rally...the list goes on.

Perhaps the final irony was that the average punter, the ones we came across every week in pubs or clubs, had little or no idea about denominations. As far as they were concerned all Christians were the same; either well meaning but misguided, or just plain mad. So while the churches expended their energy on squabbling with their neighbours, the ones who really needed to hear the message of hope remained blissfully unaware of any Gospel truth. In our years of ministry it was sad and frustrating to come across this kind of bickering, but whenever we did we always prayed that God would raise up people like James to bring fresh life and hope to tired congregations.

JESUS WANTS ME

(fast rock n roll)
I never did live a spotless life
I squandered my money and I lost a wife
Spent all my time chasing women and deals
All I wanted from life
Was a set of new wheels
Oooh wee
I knew my little black book from A to Zee
I was a real high roller the king of the scene
I was a hell of a wonderful human being
Nothing was too much trouble for me to do
As long as you were cute and female
And your eyes were blue
Oooh wee
I was a VIP with a capital V
You should have seen my clothes
You should have seen my car
Should have seen my house
(it had a mock Tudor bar)
anyone you'd met I'd known for years
anywhere you'd been I'd been before
I was cool, I was hip, I was a total bore.
The basic problem I'm sure you can see
At the center of my world was little old me
Time and again when friends came around
The sound of my voice was the only sound
Oooh wee
I was such a poseur with a capital P
Women I have known, Money I have blown
(Spent twenty years paying off the loan)
What have I achieved? What have I received?
I found out something I would never have believed
Jesus wants me for His very own!

Chapter 12: George and the Dragon

George was the kind of man you didn't mess with. Although he was no more than five feet six, short and stocky and the wrong side of fifty he was perfectly capable of ejecting an obstreperous punter twice his size through the door of his pub without breaking sweat.

To be fair I had only seen him do this twice, once at the end of an evening when a drunk had tried to grope one of the barmaids and once when a punter had called him a short fat git who didn't pull a full pint. As George explained later the short fat git part didn't bother him at all, his wife called him that twenty times a day, but he wasn't having anybody accusing him of giving short measures, he just wasn't prepared to tolerate that kind of insult in his pub.

The Black Swan stood on a roundabout on the outskirts of Glossop in Derbyshire, a smallish rather old fashioned dormitory town on the edges of Manchester and sitting at the foothills of the Pennines

I had first visited in November 1994 when it was in its heyday. George had only recently taken over the place having run a chip shop for twenty years before that and he had built it up from virtually nothing. By the time I made first contact the place was regularly heaving at weekends and live music was the order of the day. As usual I'd called in early doors before the place got too busy for the landlord to be bothered with people trying to get a gig.

It was one of those pubs that made you feel warm and comfortable as soon as you walked in, there was a lot of brassware around, mainly over the bar and plush red seating, the lighting was subdued and, at the end of the lounge, a real log fire was burning. The low hum of chatter filled the air uninterrupted by canned music (I found out later that George regarded jukeboxes as the Devil's work) and as I approached the bar George greeted me:

'Evening, chilly one in't it? What can I get you?'

This was always a tricky one, I was virtually teetotal and most landlords I'd come across had a healthy suspicion of men who drank soft drinks.

'Just a coke please.'

He didn't bat an eyelid: 'Coming right up.' I was starting to get a good feeling about this pub. I launched into my standard patter telling him we were a Christian band (I never tried to skirt round that) but didn't play hymns or choruses (a very important point to emphasize to any landlord whose sum total knowledge of Christian music had been gleaned from the thirty seconds of Songs of Praise he'd accidentally watched while looking for the footie on Sky Sports).

While he digested this information I went for the killer punch adding, as casually as possible,

'Of course we will play completely free of charge.'

I had decided as a matter of policy from day one that we would never charge for our services, accepting a gift if offered, though we would never ask for one. One of the first Christian choruses I came across shortly after my conversion had the lines:

'Freely, freely you have received,

Freely, freely give.'

That had always seemed perfectly logical to me. Nevertheless it had provoked some debate over the years with other Christian bands and performers, many of whom did charge. As was often pointed out to me I had a day job and didn't depend on the band for my income, many of them did. Fair enough, all I knew was that *not* charging was the right thing for me and I asked everyone who ever played with me to accept that as well. In the twenty odd years that Freedom played together we never wanted for a penny, having enough to cover transport, equipment, cassette and CD production, publicity and the rest all from love gifts and the sale of our music. In fact on more that one occasion we were in a position to give hundreds of pounds to ministers and churches in greater need than ourselves. It never ceased to amaze me how God was prepared to carry on producing manna from thin air when needed, even in the twentieth century.

As usual the free offer was the deal clincher and we agreed a date that we would return to play. As I turned to leave I remember that George said something that no landlord had ever said to me before...not on the first contact anyway:

'See you on the 19th, I'll looking forward to it lad.'

I also remember preparing for our first visit with an unusual amount of excitement, something inside me wanted to do George proud, I wanted to please him, to not let him down, all considerations that had never troubled me before about other landlords. As we pulled up for our first gig at the Swan George came out and started helping unload gear, another first.

November 19th 1994 was not only earth shatteringly significant because it was the first time 'Freedom' played the 'Swan' in Glossop, it also happened to be the first night of the National Lottery, a complete novelty in the UK at that time. People had been handing over their one pound in droves in the run up in full expectation that a giant finger might come down out of the sky pointing at them, accompanied by a deep giant voice saying 'It's you!'

As I came into the bar humping one of the speakers I noticed something that hadn't been there on my previous visit...a TV and it was switched on, not only that, but a crowd of excited small time gamblers were huddled round the screen all clutching their lottery cards. George must have noticed the expression on my face:

'Don't worry lad, it's a one off, as soon as draw's finished I'm knocking it off.' I breathed a sigh of relief. 'You haven't met the Mrs have you? This is Sandra, I call her the dragon, George and the dragon.' A pleasant looking woman in her mid forties emerged from the scrum round the TV, she was smiling:

'Hi...everything alright? Don't take any notice of him, he thinks he's funny.'

They both laughed, it was obvious they were comfortable with each other, a close couple.

'We're fine thanks Sandra,' I replied, 'We'll get started as soon as the lottery's finished.'

As we finished setting up I could hear the voiceover on the TV calling out the winning numbers, there was a high pitched squeal from the bar:

'I've won, I've bloody won.'

'How many numbers have you got?' demanded another, male voice, urgently.

'Three! I've won a tenner!'

'Bloody hell Viv! I thought we'd got the jackpot, I was already writing my leaving speech from t'job!'

I heard George's voice over the laughter: 'Right now come on, I'm knocking it off now, we've got a band ready to go so get yourselves in there and make 'em welcome...and no bad language...they're Christians.'

Sure enough people started to come through, sizing us up curiously in much the same way as an anthropologist would evaluate the habits of a remote South American tribe on the brink of extinction. We took full advantage of the moment starting up with a cheery ditty about paranoia, blasted out to the rhythm of the Macarena:

STRESS CITY
(to the tune and rhythm of the Macarena)
I got a semi in stress city
In a district called self pity
Worry's the game and laughs are few
At number 13 Anxious Ave.,
All my neighbours are stressed out like me

We swap paranoias over tea
We're worn out every single night
HEY PARANOIA!
Got to drop the kids and pick up my prescription
Prozac's my particular addiction
Pop a couple of tabs on the way to work
Stuck in the traffic behind some jerk
By the time I get there I'm chewing the wheel
(it's my regular morning meal)
get to the office ten minutes late
HEY PARANOIA!
Deal with problems all morning long
Accuse everybody else of being wrong
Rush out at twelve and grab a snack
Stuff it down my throat as I rush back
The phone is ringing as I walk through the door
It never rains but it pours
Boss is breathing down my neck
HEY PARANOIA!
Home from work at half past six
Dinner is coffee and a Twix
Let the dog out and close the door
Wondering what we're all here for
Got no time to talk to my wife
She is leading a separate life
Shout at the kids and start a fight
HEY PARANOIA!
Work on reports till gone midnight
Stagger to bed and switch off the light
Maybe that Jesus was right all along
When he said all this fussing and striving is wrong
I lie in bed and try to sleep
But I'm just counting a million sheep
Just as I get to a million and ten

It's time to get up and do it all again
HEY PARANOIA!

The reaction was quite humorous from our point of view, the dim light revealed faces in various stages of shock, this certainly wasn't 'Onward Christian Soldiers' or 'Rock of Ages'. As we continued with more contemporary sounding material more people drifted through, by the end of the night we were a definite hit. George came across to me as we began packing up and stuffed £100 in my hand, I protested vehemently:

'Don't worry lad,' he smiled, 'it's a lot less than I'd normally pay a band so I'm ahead on the deal.'

On the drive home I had a strong feeling that I would get to know George a lot better.

Our next visit was just before Christmas, in the meantime George had been very busy, he had had a stage put in at one end of the lounge complete with lighting and started booking cabaret acts, and he had also had an area curtained off to form a 'backstage' area. When I phoned him to confirm details he was very excited:

'I've put you on with a couple of other turns, a comedian and a knife throwing act...it's going to be a great night, something different...a Christmas special!'

I wasn't altogether convinced that we'd fit in but George was keen and I trusted him not put us in an awkward situation...I only had one question:

'Is the comedian blue?'

George laughed: 'Not in my pub lad, unless he wants to end up black and blue!'

George was bang on target when he said it would be something different, which is more than can be said for the knife thrower, who, introducing himself in a 'Red Indian' accent as 'Big Chief Sitting Bull' dressed in full Indian Chief outfit, complete with orange body tan, managed to bounce two of the knives off the board that his ageing female 'assistant' was strapped to, disastrously skimpily dressed as Hiawatha. As they came off stage to light applause the Chief pushed a ten pound note into my hand and said, in a broad Cockney accent:

'Do us a favor pal; get us a pint and a Blue Nun for the Missus.'

Next turn on was a gent who was wearing a Roman centurion's outfit over a loosely fitting string vest and Y front underpants that urgently needed changing, he introduced himself as Nero Flange. I don't remember anything of his act except the underpants, which, rather like a car crash, held a morbid fascination...every fibre of your being screamed 'Don't look, don't look!' but you just couldn't help yourself and afterwards you felt ashamed and slightly bilious.

There followed a break which we were due to follow. I sidled up to George at the bar, I wasn't quite sure what to say. He looked at me and burst out laughing:

'What a load of ****, I'll be having words with the agency. Am I glad I booked you...at least we'll have one decent turn on tonight!'

I was grateful to George for the vote of confidence, that night I think we gave the best performance we had ever given. The applause of the audience was great but I found myself peering past the spotlight to try and see if George was enjoying it, once again I was eager not to let him down.

At the end of the evening, I was in the mood to relax and talk. I chatted to George and for the first time we talked about our worries, our hopes and our beliefs. I shared with him how money was a bit tight at the moment, George told me that he had made a lot of money from the pub and from his fish and chip shop in previous years, the irony was that he was working so hard he didn't get the time to enjoy it. George described himself as a 'kind of' believer' who 'couldn't be doing with all the church stuff'. He respected my beliefs and questioned me closely about them. We talked about our wives and our families and for the first time I saw his mood darken, Sandra had just been diagnosed with breast cancer and would be starting treatment soon, he was clearly worried sick. He quickly lifted himself out of the doldrums however as he talked about his son and his love of football, then a thought seemed to occur to him:

'I have a large caravan in North Wales, beautiful van, fully kitted out on a really nice quiet site, I hardly get time to go there, why don't you take Pam down there and stay as long as you like? I can give you the keys.'

Once again I protested at his generosity but George was not the kind of man to take no for an answer. Over the next six months or so Pam and I stayed in George's caravan on several occasions and always found it a welcome break. I don't think George himself visited once during that time. 'Freedom' meantime had become regular performers at the Swan, it became almost a retreat for us where we could go and play and know that we would be treated well and listened to, in stark contrast to some of the pubs we were playing at that time where body armour and mace sprays were the order of the day.

My friendship with George continued to deepen, he was accepting and non judgmental and had the ability to make anyone who came into his pub feel as if they were one of his special customers...the original 'mine host' in fact.

Underneath the cheery exterior however I knew that George was an increasingly worried man. Sandra's health was deteriorating and she no longer came down to the bar from the flat they lived in upstairs. George fretted that the long hours he worked were keeping him from his wife, whom he adored, and who needed his help more and more. He started to speak wistfully about his days in the chip shop:

'Aye, chippy George they used to call me,' he said to me once, 'everybody knew me for miles around...chippy George.'

'They still know you George; you just serve them pints

instead of chips.'

'Aye but the hours lad, they were long, but not as long as here, Sandra used to work with me in the shop, side by side, we were a team...I miss that Scott.'

'Would you like me to pray about it George?'

'You can if you like lad.'

As things worked out the band were busy with a sudden rush of bookings in new venues for the next few months, I called George as summer was turning to autumn in 1995:

'Hi George...time for another Freedom visit?'

'Aye Scott, come when you like.'

His voice was different, I'd never heard that voice before;

'Anything the matter George?'

'She's gone lad, she passed away a couple of weeks ago.'

I felt dreadful, I had been so wrapped up in my own all important 'Freedom' schedule that I had completely forgotten about one of the few real friends the band had... in the pub world at any rate...and now it was too late, the funeral had happened and I hadn't been there for George, I didn't know what to say. George was speaking, I snapped myself back to the phone.

'When do you want to come? It'll have to be soonish mind, I've decided to sell up.'

Something inside me said 'Go to him now.'

'Can I come round today George?' The reply was immediate:

'"I'll put the kettle on.'

George and I spoke for hours that day. I felt guilty, I had let George down and I found it difficult to forgive myself. When I shared this with George he then started trying to cheer *me* up. I shouldn't feel that way, he said, look at all the times I had helped him...that counted for a lot. How was I to know what had happened? It was *his* fault for not having contacted me but what with the shock and all the arrangements...I marveled at George's ability to feel such a thing at such a time, it was then my turn to reassure him that absolutely nothing was his fault. He then asked the question I was dreading:

'But why Scott? Why Sandra? She was a good woman, never did anybody any harm, why her?'

Then, at last he lost control, he began to cry, great sobs of grief which went on and on, he covered his face with his hands, alone in his pain. He rocked gently back and forth as if trying to comfort himself, I put my arm round his shoulders, there was nothing to be said.

My mind raced back to over a decade earlier when I had been privileged enough to hear the great evangelist David Watson speak at the Free Trade Hall in Manchester. By then he was seriously ill with cancer, but, with the aid of a walking stick, insisted on standing to address the packed audience. He told us that he knew that many people had been praying for healing for him and he was worried…worried that if he was not healed that this would damage people's faith. He reminded us that what mattered was not *how long* we lived, but *how* we lived and where we were going when the journey was over. In that, he said, he had complete faith …one day he would be with his Lord and that was all that mattered to him. I shared that story with George.

I sat with George for a long time that night until he calmed down, until exhausted, he went to bed.

It was only after I left him and headed home that I realized that although I had gone there with the intention of ministering to him, in fact the opposite was true. Part of the reason I had hurried over there was to let George tell me that it was alright that I hadn't been there for him. This time, in spite of his grief, in spite of his vulnerability, George had become *my* minister.

We only played there once more after that, it wasn't the same, George's heart wasn't in it, he was busy finding a chippy he could move to. As sometimes happens in life events conspire to distract us and regrettably I lost contact with George. A year or so later I drove past the Swan to see it boarded up and deserted.

The band had lost a second home and I had lost a good friend.

When I started the music ministry, approaching pubs and clubs, it never occurred to me that I would one day be ministered to by a landlord. My spiritual arrogance was such that I couldn't imagine being taught anything by someone who had hardly opened a Bible in years. After all wasn't *I* the one who had been born again? Wasn't *I* the one who had studied the Bible? Wasn't *I* the one that God had sent out on a mission to the unsaved in the pubs and clubs? What could they possibly teach *me*?

God knew that I needed to meet somebody like George. Meeting George taught me that there are people out there who exhibit more 'Christian' qualities that many regular churchgoers do. Knowing him helped me to reassess my blinkered view of those who live in 'the world', now I knew that I had much to learn from them and that they had an enormous wealth of experience to offer.

I hope George found his chippy and rediscovered his peace of mind, I'd like to think that one day he discovered Jesus...I'm only sure of one thing, that God sent him to *me*, not the other way round and I thank God for it.

FOLLOW ME
(for George)
(slow ballad)
Well don't you know
Life is just a waiting game
Along the way
Sometimes joy, sometimes pain,
Nobody knows
Just how long we'll be here for
So waste no time,
Come and meet the man
Who can give you more.
He said:' Take my hand,
Turn around and come to me
No one can find the way
Unless he's shown by me
And I'll give you life
Just the way it ought to be
Cos the only way to have it all
Is to give it all away
And follow me.'

SOMEDAY

(slow lilting melody)
Someday we'll be with the Lord forever
The love in His heart will take us away.
Soon o so soon, yes Lord come quickly
Our life is just passing
Like a short winter's day.
High on a hill they crucified You
High in the sky you're now Lord of us all
Someday we'll be with Him for ever
The Lord of life
The Lord of light
We bless you and thank you
Dear Lord.

Chapter 13: The Community Festival

My wife, Pam, has run her own successful dancing school for over 30 years. She was a professional dancer, as was our daughter before our granddaughter arrived and so dancing and all things dancing play a major part of home life. Pam casually mentioned to me one evening that she'd been approached by a local community festival to provide some dancers for their show and why didn't 'Freedom' get involved? It would be fun.

So it was that on another wet, cold Manchester evening we showed up at the first planning meeting.

This meeting was held in one of those fairly modern smallish buildings beloved by evangelical fellowships, normally with 'witty' posters outside saying things like 'Come to church this Sunday and beat the Christmas rush!' and signs inside with exhortations such as: 'Please turn off your mobile, you don't need it to speak to God here.' Frank, the church elder, was waiting by the door to greet arrivals, he was tall and athletic with a crew cut that made him look like an American GI. At the front, smiling at everyone in general was a plump woman in her fifties who introduced herself as Dottie, she sported a dress that looked like a teepee with a head sticking through the top, she was decorated with large amounts of beads and a badge that said 'Earth, handle with care!'. The final member of the organizing group was a man in his early thirties with a pinched expression. He was carrying a canvas shoulder bag containing a filofax and a large diary stuffed with a huge amount of loose paper full of scribbled notes; this was Wayne, the rep from the Northern Arts Fund.

Dottie got things going and explained that they had been awarded a grant of £2000 by Northern Arts Fund, there was a general murmur of approval around the room, she paused to smile at Wayne who was busy picking up a pile of notes that had just dropped out of his diary onto the floor. There was, as yet an 'open agenda' for the day itself and they were open to offers and ideas. I whispered to Pam:

'Is that another way of saying they don't know what they're doing?'

A sharp dig in the ribs silenced me. Dottie continued:

'Now we're very pleased to welcome Wayne from NAF. I'm going to ask him to say a few words about how his organization can support what we're trying to do here.'

As Wayne rose to speak another huge wad of papers fell out of his diary, Dottie immediately started gathering them up, Wayne let her skivvy around him as he spoke.

'Yeah, thanks Dot, it's good to see people showing up to back their local community, to be honest we're lucky to get this money as very shortly there will be a freeze on funding further projects due to another round of government cuts.'

The last two words were said with the merest hint of a sneer:

'Of course, as with all NAF funding, funds are released retro-spectively on a match funded basis.'

One of the group who had just arrived, a goliath of a man with muscles on his muscles, spoke up in a broad Liverpudlian accent.

'Excuse me la' but what does that mean in English?'

Wayne cast a weary look at him:

'It means you don't get £2000 unless you raise £2000 yourself.'

I noticed that the smile on Dottie's face had taken on a slightly frozen quality.

'And how are we supposed to raise £2000? This is a working class community, we don't all live in Didsbury you know.'

I assumed that our latecomer friend had the inside dope on Wayne as a secret Didsbury dweller, one of Manchester's trendiest suburbs, of course the fact that Richard and Judy, a very 'right on' couple who hosted a popular daytime TV show lived there had forever destroyed its street cred in the minds of many.

Dot intervened quickly:

'I'm so glad you asked that question,' she lied, 'that's exactly what we're holding this meeting for, we need ideas, ideas, ideas!!'

The match funding revelation had put a bit of a damper on the proceedings, so there was a temporary lull in the bright idea department. A very small old lady sitting in the corner, who hadn't said anything up to this point, suddenly came to life:

'Why don't we have a Whist drive?'

There was a terrible silence.

'Or perhaps a jumble sale?'

Another painful silence ensued.

'Or we could combine the two, a jumble sale in the afternoon followed by a whist drive?'

'I'll give you one thing,' I thought to myself admiringly, 'you're not a quitter.'

Frank chipped in:

'I'm afraid that if you were proposing holding the whist drive here that would pose a problem as Reverend Rodger doesn't approve of gambling activities on the premises.'

'What about the raffle he holds every year at the Christmas mix 'n mingle?' asked a woman sat immediately behind him.

The GI rounded on her 'That's quite different Lois, that's held in the Army Cadet hut.'

Dot joined the fray:

'Perhaps the best thing is for all of us to go away and have a good think and bring ideas to next week's meeting. Now, moving on…has anybody got any talents or skills they can offer?'

By the end of the meeting Pam's dancing school had been signed up, as had 'Freedom' together with various other enter-tainments. The latecomer built like an Olympic weightlifter turned out to be, to the amazement of all, the proprietor of 'Uncle Chris's Doggy World', a children's travelling show. It was agreed that there would be further planning meetings in the run up to the event itself which was set for a Sunday in three months time. I couldn't help wondering if getting involved in this venture was the right thing to do for the band. We were, after all, an evangelical outfit whose purpose was to win souls for Christ, not a schedule filler between a whist drive and somersaulting poodles. Would appearing in such a line up somehow 'cheapen' or trivialize the Gospel message we were trying to convey I wondered? Over the coming weeks as the event started to take shape this question became more and more pressing in my mind.

Over the years 'Freedom' took many forms, ranging from a seven piece vocal ensemble to a four piece rock band to a duo, right now it was a duo. My current singing partner, a Nigerian girl called Dorike, was one of those Christians that sees good in everybody and everything and trusts God completely and who therefore has no place in the traditional church. Her exalted level of spirituality often left me tagging along breathless in her wake; at one of our regular rehearsals I shared my misgivings with her. Her reaction was predictably simple:

'There's going to be an audience isn't there?'

'Right.'

'Nobody's told you that we can't preach the Gospel have they?'

'No.'

'We've got the kind of music that they will like to hear 'cos we've played it successfully at similar non Christian events haven't we?'

'Right.'

'Isn't this just the kind of audience you formed the band to reach, whether they're in a pub or a club or they've come for an afternoon out?'

'Right.'

'So who is giving us the authority to turn down such a God given opportunity?'

There's just no arguing with that kind of remorseless spirit-filled logic.

Somehow, and I can't really remember just how, the group managed to raise just short of the target £2000. At the final planning meeting I was surprised to see that Wayne was missing, apparently, according to Dot, he'd left NAF at very short notice and taken a job in the Gay village, as I looked at Pam we both said in perfect unison:

'Government cuts.'

Fortunately the promised funds had not also left with Wayne and there was money to pay for staging, land hire and the thousand and one items needed to make such an event work. We hired a flat open sided lorry as one of the stages, this would be the stage for 'Freedom' and would be driven on site early in the morning as it was too expensive to hire for two days. I had not had time to visit the site itself which was a local park but was assured that there would be no problem.

The night before the great day a huge cloudburst brought torrential rain which lasted until dawn. As we emerged into the dripping wet early morning alarm bells were ringing in my head. Sure enough when I arrived on site I was met by a group of volunteers who were standing around watching an enormous truck slip and slither in deep mud, trying to get over an incline in the grass to where it was supposed to be. I walked round to the driver's cab to be met by a red faced individual leaning out of the door window. He shared his concerns:

'There's no f ****** way this f****** truck is going to get up that f****** hill!'

In case I hadn't understood the problem fully he offered some clarification:

'The f******* mud is too f****** deep, if you ask me I'm wasting my f****** time. Whoever thought this up is a right f******* numpty. The best thing I can do is back up and try and park in the f******* car park. At least it's f******* hard standing there.'

I agreed and so, accompanied by further outbursts of expletives, the truck was slowly reversed to the small car park at the entrance to the park. Just as the driver turned off the engine I spotted some kind of official wearing a peaked cap limping towards us at incredible speed, he was waving his arms around:

'Oi, Oi Oi...you can't leave that here, this is a car park not a lorry park.'

Out of the corner of my eye I saw the lorry driver just beginning to form a word beginning with F, I managed to get in first.

'This lorry is one of the stages for the festival but we can't get it across the park because of the mud, so unfortunately it's going to have to go here.'

The park keeper looked at me, then the truck driver, then back at me...then back at the lorry driver, then back at me. I noticed he had a twitch in his right eye, the twitch obviously extended to his brain, he seemed to come to a decision and pointed at the truck:

'You can't leave that here, this is a car park not a lorry park.'

The truck driver and I exchanged glances, then he decided to express himself:

'F*** me!'

The parky drew himself up to the maximum height his gammy leg would allow, but he was listing to port by at least twenty degrees:

'There's no need for that kind of language, now get it shifted.' The twitch was now out of control.

At that point the cavalry arrived in the shape of Dottie, she spoke directly to our inclined friend:

'Now then Bill what's the problem?'

Within two minutes she had sent him on his way, noticing our astonishment she explained,

'Bill and I go back years, he used to have a bit of a thing for me at one time,' she chuckled.

'So can you play here?' she asked.

'I suppose so,' I said, 'as long as the generator shows up we can play more or less anywhere. My mind scurried back to a field at the Crossfire festival some years before.'

As the morning wore on to our huge relief the sun decided to come out and start to dry things up. Many of the people who had showed up wearing trainers or sandals however thought better of ruining their footgear in the mud and contented themselves with staying in the one place where it was reasonably mud free...the car park. We had a ready made audience and made the most of it. I was in a mood to celebrate and so Dorike and I gave our best rendition of one of our songs tailored for the mass market...

LIVING YOUR LIFE LIKE A LIE
(bluegrass beat)
I worked damn hard to get where I am today
What's mine is mine, being soft don't pay
Don't forget nothing in life is free
Look after number one, that's my mentality.
It's all aboard the merry go round
Leave your soul in the lost and found
Find your place in the sun (looking after number one)
It's all aboard the merry go round
Don't stop to think where you're bound
Living your life like a lie...it only stops when you die.
I got a job and started to settle down
Wasn't my fault I couldn't stop playing around
You're only young once, so get what you can while it's there
And believe me boys I was getting my share.
The company did what was right by me
But I fiddled expenses and got plenty of perks tax free
Yep life was sweet, because my friends you see,
The meaning of life is financial security.

We were thrilled that things had taken such an unexpected turn for the better...better, in fact, than we could ever have hoped for on a dry sunny day when the crowds would have been dispersed across the whole of the park and we would have had the attention of a tenth of the numbers that we did.

Needless to say elsewhere things weren't going so well.

Pam's dancers were slipping around on the sodden wooden flats that had been put down as their stage in front of an audience limited to the hard core posse of mothers that were always prepared to walk through fire to see their little darlings perform. Uncle Chris abandoned his mission when his group of snow white poodles decided it would be fun to roll around in the mud and suddenly became the black sheep of the festival.

Meanwhile, back in the car park things were in full swing, the crowd, fuelled up with the cut price burgers and hotdogs from the waterlogged vans, not to mention certain beverages brought over from the pub across the road, were in a party mood. We played rock n roll, Gospel swing and jazz until we could play no more and they loved it. Much more important than that though was the interest it generated in what we were about, as I made sure that in my patter between numbers I made our message clear.

We were exhausted but exhilarated by the end of the afternoon. God had done what he is so very good at...pulling victory out of seeming defeat. So much of Jesus' ministry was about that very thing, whether it was saving the day at a wedding by coming up with more wine, or saving the necks of his disciples by calming a storm, He put things right.

That Sunday in the car park convinced me, once and for all, that God really *does* have a plan for us, which so often we don't understand until *after* the event...sometimes years after. As Paul wrote in 1 Corinthians 13 'now we see in a mirror, dimly, but then face to face. Now I know only in part, then I will know fully'.

MARTHA'S SONG

Sunday morning, the nightmare Friday
Like fresh blood running in my eyes.
Now too late, too late to tell Him I'm sorry.
Sorry for complaining about work
While my sister sat at his feet.
Sorry for not believing
Until the day my brother staggered from the tomb,
The moment when I finally knew
Sorry that it's too late,
Too late to tell Him I loved Him.
Slowly dawn breaks over the city
Ending the hopeless night
and His disciples
Skulking in shadows, alone with their fear
But slowly the sun rises
New clean light in the world.
I have a strange feeling inside
Like a fresh start, not an ending,
As if suddenly,
All over the world
A million broken hearts are mending.

Chapter 14: The Attraction of the Unexpected

Over a twenty year period of slogging our way round the highways and byways of northern England I think it's fair to say that we gave quite a few people a surprise. From the moment we turned up at a pub gig we didn't really have anything to lose. Most people's stereotyped image of Christians and, in particular, Christian music, was so negative that we could have played just about anything and, as long as it wasn't 'Onward Christian Soldiers' or 'Jesus wants me for a sunbeam' it would be received with a huge sigh of relief and possibly even applause.

When I added into the mix a bit of humorous backchat between numbers, the relief of the audience would often start to transmogrify into genuine warmth. Most people didn't know, of course, that humor amongst Christians had been forbidden by the Council of Nicaea in 325 AD. Nevertheless the idea of a Christian actually cracking gags in a public place held the same shock factor for many as if it was discovered that the meat pies they bought at the bar actually contained any meat.

We knew this and made it work for us, many of our lyrics were relentlessly 'unChristian' we sang about old blokes called Stan who tried it on with the home help, about stressed out executives popping pills on the way to work and fiddling their expenses and about smooth guys chatting up women. These lyrics spoke to the old chap sat in the corner with his pint, to the group of young men down for the night to see what they could find, to the middle class, middle aged man sitting nursing his scotch with his wife wishing he was with someone else.

The music sounded like a lot of stuff that would normally burp out of the jukebox on a Saturday night, it was a mix of rock n'roll; reggae, electric funk, ballad, anything in fact that didn't sound like a hymn.

The combination of contemporary lyrics set to pop tunes and introduced by a gag cracking band member was our passport into venues that would normally go into catatonic shock at the mere idea of booking a bunch of Christians to provide an evening's entertainment.

Of course there was a downside to this, for, just as our approach endeared us to the pubs and clubs and some of the more evangelical churches, so it also closed some doors in our faces. These doors, it must be said, normally belonged to the more traditional churches who didn't see any need for that kind of thing and viewed it with a certain amount of suspicion. These were also the churches that in the main (and I say this with no smugness or critical edge but merely as a statement of fact) had elderly dwindling congregations. Still there's room for us all in God's kingdom.

We were always careful to be as unchristian as possible, and for unchristian don't read unbeliever, read *un organized religion*. Time and time again in our conversations with the ordinary folk who populate our pubs and clubs the one reason quoted for unbelief or scepticism was 'The Church'…that great traditional edifice that so many people saw as a block between them and God. These people wanted the common touch, a message that spoke to them in language they could understand in a way that was familiar. In clubland it was pop music with meaningful lyrics, in Jesus' time, in an agricultural society, it was stories about corn and sheep and fish that had a deeper meaning. We were simply following His example.

'Freedom' finally disbanded in 2007 after nearly twenty five years on the road without a record deal or chart entry to our name. We had made a career out of being unsigned but right through that long journey we knew that, though we might still be unsigned, we certainly weren't unloved, in fact we had been loved from day one by the same Lord that we sought to glorify.

It's the good news of the Gospel; God has a special place in His heart for the 'unsigned' ones among us and He loves us and blesses us and uses us just as much as anyone else. We are the ones, after all, that Jesus chose to spend his time with and it was people like us, ordinary working people, that he chose to be his disciples. The key for us in Freedom was constantly turning to Him for support and strength and if you, gentle reader, were ever considering doing anything so radical as taking the Gospel to places it isn't normally heard, He will be your strength too.

If you would like to receive further information on the author, his ongoing ministry and his music, including how to access free samples of 'Freedom' tracks, please e mail

saturdaynightbeliever@yahoo.co.uk.

A PRAYER TO YOU

Let's pretend love's an easy thing
Holding the world on the end of its golden string
Let's pretend the world has come of age
Preferring peace to the fanatic's rage
Let's pretend life's sure
Cos we can't take the truth anymore.
Let's pretend we always seek a person's mind
Paying no heed to their religion, class or kind
Let's pretend passion's a thing of the past
Where wise men always see sense at last
Let's pretend there are no goodbyes
When nobody mourns and nobody cries.
Let's pretend we all give ourselves to each other
Holding back nothing, all equal, all our brother's brother.
Let's pretend death never tears us apart
Where life is lived with a gentle heart
Let's pretend right always wins
Where the world's a place free from sin
Let's pretend life's sure
Cos we can't take the truth anymore
This is a prayer to you
Hold us now, help us now
This is a prayer to you
Father of us all.
This is a prayer to you
Lead us now, guide us now
This is a prayer to you
Save us once again.

Appendix 1
How to use subliminal message techniques to secure a gig

Important note

This script has been honed and polished to perfection over the years and should not be altered in any way. It may be used in person, or, preferably on the phone which means it can be read with no need to memorize. It is crucial to keep talking without interruption.

Hi, sorry I'm calling/visiting late I couldn't get free any earlier, I tried to call but unfortunately my mobile had no charge. Free time is in such short supply these days. My name is….. (insert your name here)…… and I want to talk to you about my band called Freedom (NB having the word 'free' contained in the title is a major advantage). We are a Christian band that plays in pubs and clubs everywhere, all over the free world in fact! We've freed up some time in our busy schedule to play some gigs in this area and wonder if you might be interested (and you may speak freely). Sorry for asking, but that music in the background, is it 'Alright Now' by Free? Certainly sounds like it, anyway, where was I? We don't try and force our beliefs on people…it's a free world after all and we can handle any verbals from customers pretty well, in fact we believe in freedom of speech. After all, without freedom where would we be? Our music isn't churchy, it's basically pop with Christian lyrics so don't worry it's hymn free!
So if you're interested and have some slots free perhaps you might like to book us.
By the way did I mention we play for free?

NB If no gig is secured as a result of this technique your listener is either stone deaf or Grand Master of the local Hellfire club… otherwise positive results are guaranteed.

Appendix 2
Ten survival tips for pub ministry

1. Avoid walking up to large bald gentlemen with muscles and tattoos and asking: "Hello friend, do you have a personal relationship with the Lord Jesus Christ?"

2. If the same large bald gentleman with muscles and tattoos offers a critique of your music such as, 'a load of f****** s***!' try to adopt a facial expression that says: 'I don't exactly agree with you there friend but, on the other hand, that is one of the wittiest and most original comments I've heard in years.'

3. If witnessing one to one with a member of the opposite sex, keep a sharp eye out for a partner with possessiveness issues.

4. If female and witnessing one to one with a male, avoid any invitations back to his place for further 'Bible study'.

5. Avoid potential aggro such as laughing and joking loudly during Bingo, eating the last meat pie or suggesting to the regulars that perhaps twenty pints a night might be a tad excessive.

6. Fight fire with fire...so when you've been earholed by the pub bore on how much his allotment rent has gone up, get involved! Exactly *how* much has it gone up? What can be done about it? Does this mean the end of allotments as we know them? Keep up this up until he's ready to submit and talk about something else...like Jesus for example.

7. If possible dress to fit in. A man turning up at a working men's club sporting a bright pink T shirt with the logo: 'Discover your female side' probably isn't going to get quite the reaction he was hoping for.

8. Avoid the terrors of churchspeak...phrases such as 'you must be born again'; 'He was made a living sacrifice for us all' and 'we've been washed in His blood' sound rather gory to the unchurched ear. This is not to say however that your average northern pub regular has no command of languages. On the contrary, continued churchspeak will result in you being given a demo of fluent Anglo Saxon.

9. Allow yourself to be imperfect...nothing gets the punter's back up more than talking to somebody who's adopting a slightly patronising tone. Jesus had a handy word for people like this...Pharisees.

10. When packing up and loading heavy gear at the end of a long night take full advantage of anyone who offers to help (rare but not unknown), this is no time for Christian selflessness.

Appendix 3
Ten things not to say during a pub gig on a Saturday night

1. This next song was inspired by the French Monastic Taize community...

2. Kum Ba Ya my Lord, Kum Ba Ya...all together now!

3. Would anybody like to join us in our quiet time later on?

4. Now I need two volunteers for this next section, one to hold the felt board and the other to hand me the puppets.

5. Of course I'm a Methodist which means we don't really approve of alcohol.

6. We believe that nobody is beyond salvation, no matter how rough or terribly deprived the background they come from, which is why we're here tonight.

7. Would all you bald gentlemen with tattoos at the bar mind keeping the noise down please? Some people are trying to listen.

8. This next song is a modernized version of an old John Wesley hymn. John Wesley was a fascinating man, let me tell you all about him...

9. We're finishing off with a Bible Quiz tonight so don't rush off.

10. Any requests?

Appendix 4
Handy glossary of terms

For those about to set out into the challenging world of frontline music ministry I offer this brief guide which may help you avoid confusion, misunderstanding or possible violence.

Top Ten Pub landlord / Concert Secretary terminology

Original	Translation
Yes we like to give unknown bands a chance now and again	You're not being paid
It's normally 'free and easy' night the night you're coming	Can you play 'My way' and 'The Birdie Song' at least twenty times in one night?
It's a lively crowd in tonight	Are you wearing a box?
Bingo starts at 7.30pm	Don't even think of playing between 7.30 and 8pm
So what kind of music do you play?	If it's hymns or choruses forget it
You'll find that 99% of folk we get in here are pretty easy going and broadminded.	Watch out for the 1% that'll put you in traction

Not many in tonight

You're not being paid

All of your stuff's original then is it?

I'm sticking the
jukebox back on

I thought you'd prefer to play in
the lounge

The big match is on
big Screen TV
in the main bar

That was certainly a change
from our normal stuff

You're not being paid
and you're not
coming back

Top Ten Church minister/ elder terminology

Original	Translation
I've had a word from the Lord about tonight…	Don't even think about contradicting me
We've publicized your visit widely	It was announced once in the notices last Sunday
I've prepared a running order	You'll be doing one song as people leave
I'll leave the content entirely up to you	I won't be there
Will you be doing well known choruses?	The overhead projector's broken

We have a really active music group

I've let them do most
of the music to keep
the peace

Will it be a long service/concert?

The Ring n Ride's
booked for 9.30pm

We're hoping for a good
turn out tonight

I've told them it's free

We'll be having the hotpot
during the interval

Make sure you
do your best stuff
before they all leave
after the food

If you want to sell tapes or CDs
that's no problem

You're not being paid

Appendix 5
Ten things not to say during a traditional church service

1. Good Morning/Evening are you ready to dance and sing and shout for the Lord?

2. This next song was inspired by a prostitute I met in the pub.

3. Does anybody feel moved by the Spirit to give us their testimony/ give us their prophecy/speak in tongues?

4. Some of the band have used drugs in the past and we'd like to sing about that now.

5. Let's all greet one another with the kiss of peace.

6. We are very pleased to have been invited to minister to you in such a beautiful old building, normally, of course, we play in pubs and clubs.

7. This next song is written in big band 40's swing style so should sound familiar.

8. We've chosen a wide selection of brand new choruses for this service and we're going to learn them together.

9. Sing up!

(For evening services only)
10. It looks like we might overrun a little and finish after 7.30…that's OK isn't it?

BOOKS

O is a symbol of the world, of oneness and unity. In different cultures it also means the "eye," symbolizing knowledge and insight. We aim to publish books that are accessible, constructive and that challenge accepted opinion, both that of academia and the "moral majority."

Our books are available in all good English language bookstores worldwide. If you don't see the book on the shelves ask the bookstore to order it for you, quoting the ISBN number and title. Alternatively you can order online (all major online retail sites carry our titles) or contact the distributor in the relevant country, listed on the copyright page.

See our website **www.o-books.net** for a full list of over 500 titles, growing by 100 a year.

And tune in to myspiritradio.com for our book review radio show, hosted by June-Elleni Laine, where you can listen to the authors discussing their books.

MySpiritRadio